Steve Tasker's
TALES FROM THE BUFFALO BILLS

Steve Tasker
with Scott Pitoniak

SP
SPORTS
PUBLISHING
L.L.C.

SportsPublishingLLC.com

ISBN-10: 1-59670-092-0
ISBN-13: 978-1-59670-092-5

Publishers: Peter L. Bannon and Joseph J. Bannon Sr.
Senior managing editor: Susan M. Moyer
Acquisitions editor: Bob Snodgrass
Developmental editor: Mark Newton
Art director: K. Jeffrey Higgerson
Dust jacket design: Heidi Norsen
Interior layout: Kathryn R. Holleman
Photo editor: Erin Linden-Levy

Sports Publishing L.L.C.
804 North Neil Street
Champaign, IL 61820
Phone: 1-877-424-2665
Fax: 217-363-2073
SportsPublishingLLC.com

Printed in the United States of America

Library of Congress Cataloging-in-Publication Data

Tasker, Steve, 1962-
Steve Tasker's tales from the Buffalo Bills / Steve Tasker ; with Scott Pitoniak.
    p. cm.
  ISBN-13: 978-1-59670-092-5 (alk. paper)
  ISBN-10: 1-59670-092-0 (alk. paper)
  1. Buffalo Bills (Football team)--History. I. Pitoniak, Scott. II. Title.
GV956.B83T37 2006
796.332'640974797--dc22
                        2006021931

CONTENTS

FOREWORD

During my years playing in the National Football League, I had the opportunity to compete with and against scores of talented athletes. Many of them were close teammates who understood and shared my passion for playing the game we loved. There was one, however, who stood out as a leader, an athlete, a great family man, and a great friend—Steve Tasker, or "Seve" as all of his close friends referred to him.

At training camp with the Bills, Steve was a player no one wanted to cover or could cover, for that matter. All the defensive backs would challenge each other to see how they would fare against his speed and toughness. Nobody touched him. This was not exclusive to our team; it happened around the league.

He excelled in special teams play in the NFL. In fact, teams game-planned around Steve. You could see how they would have him double covered, and if that didn't work, a third guy would peel off to try to stop Steve's progress. But we know that wasn't possible—he played with heart, soul, and a determination unmatched by many players today. He could see the field and the openings better than anyone. He could find the player with the ball and make a hit that no one would forget.

Everyone knows of his success on special teams, but what they don't know is that I think he could have been one of the best wide receivers to play the game. I lobbied hard with the coaches to include Steve in our offense and design plays with his ability in mind. They went along to a certain point but didn't want to pull him from special teams. That was a shame—his numbers could have been as good as those of someone like Steve Largent.

I will never forget that at each and every game, Steve and I would wait in the tunnel, shoulder to shoulder. We would walk onto the field, proud to be a part of the Buffalo Bills. But at Super Bowl XXV, as we stood in the tunnel at one of the greatest games of our lives, the hair went up on the back of our necks. We could feel the rippling effect of the band, the crowd, and the energy. We walked out, and there were the flashes of cameras everywhere. I will always remember it as one of the best trips we took as teammates down the tunnel.

When I reflect on that time in our lives, I know that it was not only his talent and ability on the field that impressed me but how he conducted himself off the field. Steve has always been a great family man and understands what is important in life—family.

It was an honor to play with "Seve" and an even greater honor to call him my friend.

–Jim Kelly
Pro Football Hall of Fame Quarterback

ACKNOWLEDGMENTS

The authors would like to thank Sarah Tasker for her meticulous copyediting; developmental editors Mark Newton and Elisa Bock Laird of Sports Publishing LLC for their guidance on this project; photographers Jamie Germano and Bill Wippert; Tom Flynn and the Rochester, New York, *Democrat and Chronicle*; Bob Snodgrass; graphic designers Heidi Norsen and Kayte Holleman; and Buffalo Bills legend Jim Kelly.

INTRODUCTION

Before kickoffs, during our Super Bowl years in the early 1990s, coach Marv Levy would gather us together in a team huddle and shout, "Where would you rather be than right here, right now?"

No response was necessary, because we all knew exactly where we wanted to be: right there, right then, playing football for Marv and the Buffalo Bills.

I had the privilege to spend 12 seasons with the Bills, and they were 12 of the most exhilarating, memorable years of my life. Yeah, we may not have won a Super Bowl, but we did establish ourselves as one of the most resilient sports teams of all-time. Our four consecutive title-game appearances remain unprecedented, as does our comeback from a 32-point second-half deficit.

Although we came up empty in the big game, I would do it all over again in a heartbeat if I could—as long I could do it with those same guys I played with and for on those great Bills teams.

It's funny I say that now, because I didn't have any warm, fuzzy feelings when I heard the Bills picked me up off waivers from the Houston Oilers midway through the 1986 season. In fact, I initially thought I was the victim of some cruel joke.

Back then, being acquired by Buffalo was akin to being sentenced to prison in Siberia. See, the Bills were the laughingstock of the National Football League at the time. They had been bad seemingly forever. They were coming off consecutive 2-14 seasons, and despite the presence of potentially great young players such as Jim Kelly, Bruce Smith, and Andre Reed, things didn't look like they were going to get better any time soon.

Plus, everybody had heard the stories about Buffalo's notoriously bad weather. The perception around the league was that it snowed there in July.

I remember getting ready for practice at the Oilers training complex one day in early November 1986 when our coach, Jerry Glanville, said I had a phone call. The guy on the other end of the line said he was Bo Shempley from the Buffalo Bills, and he told me the team had just claimed me off waivers. He asked whether my agent had contacted me, and I said, "No, he hasn't, because I don't have an agent."

My heart began racing. I had been caught totally off guard. I had been on the injured reserve list for several weeks and was healthy again, and the Oilers placed me on waivers so they could activate me for that Sunday's game. I quickly called my wife, Sarah, to tell her the news and asked her to call my parents right away because they were planning to come to Houston to watch me play that Sunday.

After I hung up, I headed to the locker room to clean out my stuff, and one of our safeties, Jeff Donaldson, came up to me wearing this huge grin. He told me the call wasn't real and that one of the guys had disguised his voice to play a prank on me. So I ran back and called Sarah to tell her that it was all a joke. She phoned my parents to tell them they should come to Houston that weekend after all.

That evening Sarah and I went out and bought all these groceries in anticipation of my folks' visit, and when we returned home, there a bunch of messages on my answering machine.

The first message was from some guy named Bill Polian, and he said he was from the Bills and that it was imperative I get back to him ASAP. I immediately wondered if the guys were jerking my chain again, but the voice sounded real.

I played the second message, and it was Polian again. There was an even greater sense of urgency in his voice. He said they needed to get me to Buffalo right away because they wanted to play me in Sunday's game.

The third message was from Glanville, and he said I needed to call him right away.

The fourth message was from Bills punter John Kidd, who was my roommate at Northwestern University. He wanted to welcome me to Buffalo.

I called Glanville, and he confirmed that the Bills had indeed claimed me; that this was no joke. He tried to persuade me to deliberately flunk the physical the Bills would give me so that I could be reclaimed by the Oilers. I considered it but ultimately decided that I had to tell the truth.

Early the next morning, I found myself on a plane to Buffalo, pondering my future. One day, I'm a second-year, fringe player coming off a knee injury, just settling in with the Oilers. Then, in a matter of hours, everything had changed. A cruel joke had become reality. I'd been sentenced to that prison in Siberia.

I arrived in Buffalo Saturday afternoon, and the Bills medical staff put me through some tests to make sure my knee was sound. While I was sitting there in my underwear, Levy walked in to introduce himself. I felt some familiarity with him because, growing up in Kansas, I had been a huge Chiefs fan, and Marv had coached there for several years.

At the team meeting that night, Marv introduced me, and I got up sheepishly and waved. Jim Kelly and Bruce Smith and Fred Smerlas were there, and there I was, a 5 foot, 9 inch, 180-pound white guy who looked like a 15-year-old. I could tell that these guys were wondering to themselves, "We're a 2-14 team, and this is the kind of guy they are bringing in to make us better?"

The next day, I went over to the stadium for the game against Pittsburgh with John, and while we were walking toward the locker room, he introduced me to linebacker Jim Haslett. After I got my ankles taped, Jim walked over to me and said, "Dude, I'm sorry. When John introduced me to you, I was going to tell you that nobody but players are allowed in the locker room before a game. I didn't know you were a player."

I told him not to worry because I was mistaken for a ball boy all the time.

That game wound up being the Bills' debut for both me and Marv. I'll never forget it, because it was sunny and mild, and the wind gusts approached 45 miles per hour. The gales were so powerful they blew the hats off several members of the marching band who were performing the anthem.

I played special teams against the Steelers that day, and it didn't take long for me to record my first tackle as a Bill. But it wasn't exactly what I had in mind. I was back for the opening kickoff return with Eric Richardson. He coughed up the ball, and I had to tackle the Steeler who recovered it. One play, and we already were in the hole. I was thinking, "No wonder this team has been 2-14."

But the day actually turned out to be a good one for us: we ground out a 16–12 victory. Although we struggled the remainder of that season, I could sense something special was about to unfold. Kelly and Bruce and Andre were better than advertised—Hall of Famers in the making. And Marv, with the assistance of owner Ralph Wilson and Polian, was the perfect leader to transform us from doormats to champions.

The other thing I sensed right away was that Buffalo was a great place to live and raise a family. The people are down to earth and big-hearted. And, boy, do they love their football.

It's funny how things work out in life. If you had asked me back in November 1986 where I would rather be, I would have answered, "Any place but Buffalo."

But as I discovered, perception isn't always reality. You can't always judge a book by its cover.

I'm so happy that prank came true, and I'm honored that I was the first personnel move Marv made as Bills coach, because there was no place that I would rather have been during my football career than right there, right then, playing ball for him and the Buffalo Bills.

ARCHITECTS OF SUCCESS: MARV, RALPH, AND BILL

PROFESSOR MARV

Playing for Marv definitely was an educational experience. Our knowledge of football wasn't the only thing that expanded. Our Harvard-educated coach was first and foremost a teacher, and during his talks he occasionally threw out some ten-dollar, multisyllabic words that had guys scratching their heads. Kent Hull joked that his vocabulary increased tenfold while playing for Marv. Kent said you needed a dictionary and a thesaurus in addition to your playbook at team meetings.

A history book would have helped too.

Marv loved quoting Winston Churchill and FDR. He often used World War II analogies to drive his points home. Once, before we embarked on a stretch of three straight road games, Marv went into this five-minute speech about how Germany was the world's powerhouse at the start of World War II in 1941. He mentioned how they had the best-trained soldiers, the most destructive weapons, and the most disciplined leaders. But three years later, Berlin was in ruins and the German army was on the run. He said there was only one explanation for their failure: Germany couldn't win on the road.

His point was that we might be dominant at home, but if we didn't prove we could win our away games, we weren't going to realize our ultimate goals.

We all got a kick out of his stories and how he made them relevant to our situation.

After he gave us a talk about Germany's overconfidence in World War II and the importance of crossing one river at a time like Hannibal, Marv joked to a reporter: "To be honest, I don't know how many of these guys even know what World War II was, and they probably think Hannibal is an offensive tackle for the Jets."

"MARVISMS"

Marv had many sayings. Some were corny; some were quite profound. Before games, we would huddle around him, and he'd ask: "Where would you rather be than right here, right now?"

It became his signature phrase and the title of his best-selling autobiography.

Here are several of my favorite "Marvisms":

- "If Michelangelo had wanted to play it safe, he would have painted the floor of the Sistine Chapel."
- "What you do should speak so loudly that no one can hear what you say."
- "Adversity is an opportunity for heroism."
- "World War II was a must-win."
- "Expect rejection, but expect more to overcome it."
- "The coach who starts listening to the fans winds up sitting next to them."

LEARNING FROM THE MASTER

The second week I was with the team, Marv spent 45 minutes with me one snowy day after practice, demonstrating how to block punts. He was in his early 60s at the time, but that didn't stop him from getting down in a stance and showing me the path to take off the corner.

Marv had begun his NFL career coaching special teams for the Washington Redskins under George Allen, so he had it down to a science. He taught me how it was always seven steps to the block point and said I should go in low and try to take the ball off the punter's foot without flinching.

That Sunday we went to New England to play the Patriots, and I wound up blocking a punt to set up a field goal. As I jogged to the sideline after the block, I pointed at Marv, and he smiled back at me. We connected. From that moment on, I was Marv's guy. The block showed him that I was coachable and that I was really into special teams and willing to do what it took to be successful. That was really important to Marv, because he was one of the first coaches to realize that special teams accounted for a third of the plays in a football game, so you had better be good at it.

MARV THE LYRICIST

One time before we played the Dolphins, Marv came up to us and said, "I'll tell you what. I don't particularly care for the rap music I hear in the locker room, but if you guys win, I'll sing a rap song in front of the team next week."

The thought of this white-haired, 60-something guy singing a rap song seemed comical to us. Let's just say it wasn't the greatest incentive Marv ever gave us before a game.

Well, we went out there and beat the Dolphins, and the next week, when we were in the team meeting, Marv handed out these sheets with a bunch of lyrics on them. He told us it was a fight song rather than a rap song he'd composed, and he invited us to sing along with him. Marv loved college fight songs, so he had taken the time to write one about the Bills. It was an awful song, but it was hilarious watching him sing it to us. It was just another case of him showing his human side, and another reason why we all loved the guy so much.

MARV'S BOUT WITH PROSTATE CANCER

I thought the four Super Bowl losses were painful, but they seemed trivial compared to the news we received from Marv on October 16, 1995—the day after we had beaten Seattle to improve to 5-1. At a team meeting at Rich Stadium that morning, Marv told us that he would be leaving the Bills

Marv Levy addresses the media before Super Bowl XXV.
Photo courtesy of the Rochester Democrat and Chronicle

temporarily to undergo surgery for the removal of his cancerous prostate. He said that the prognosis was good and that he would be back in six weeks or less. Still, despite his reassurances, the announcement hit us like a ton of bricks. We were really concerned about him. Yeah, Marv was in great shape, but he was close to 70 at the time, and this wasn't some minor operation he was about to undergo. This was serious stuff.

Before he left, Marv told us that Elijah Pitts would be the head coach in his absence and that we should treat Eli as we would him. That wouldn't be an issue because Eli was beloved and respected by everyone on the team. He had come from Philander Smith, a small college in Little Rock, Arkansas, and had carved out a respectable pro playing career for himself as a running back with Vince Lombardi's Green Bay Packers. The highlight of his career occurred when he scored two touchdowns for the Pack in the very first Super Bowl against the Kansas City Chiefs (a Chiefs team, that, by the way, featured our defensive coordinator, Walt Corey, at linebacker).

After he retired as a player, Eli began a long and distinguished career as an NFL assistant. He was a sincere, even-keeled, fair-minded guy with a great sense of humor and a booming voice that was as deep as Barry White's. The guys all wanted so badly to do well for Eli and for Marv during this difficult stretch, but, in retrospect, we may have tried too hard.

The good news was that Marv recovered more quickly than anyone could have imagined and was back coaching after missing just three games.

The bad news was that we lost two of those games.

The first of those defeats occurred in a Monday night game in New England a week after Marv had dropped his bombshell. I'll never forget that game because Eli had asked me to address the team before we headed out of the locker room. It was the only pregame speech I ever gave.

I told my teammates, "There is a special guy in Orchard Park who will be watching us tonight, and all of us are here because he chose us to be on this team. Tonight we have a chance to go out there and show the whole world that he made the right choice when he chose Eli to fill in for him and that he made the right choice when he chose us to play for him. Let's go."

I thought I had nailed it pretty good. We went charging out of that locker room in Foxboro, Massachusetts, like a stampede of buffaloes.

What I quickly discovered is that pregame speeches are good until you line up for that first kickoff. Then you have to back your words and emotions up with actions. We wound up getting spanked by the Patriots 27–14 in front of a national television audience. Nobody ever asked me to address the team again before a game, and I was glad.

It's hard to describe the emotions we felt when Marv returned in November. I remember us giving him a round of applause when he showed up for his first team meeting after resuming his full-time duties. It was good to see him back where he belonged. We felt like our family was whole again. Everything seemed right with our world.

As I said, the only disappointment was going 1-2 under Eli. I always felt Eli deserved a shot as a full-time head coach in the NFL, and, although he interviewed for jobs several times, he never got the big break. Sadly, Eli died of cancer a few years later. We all miss him. He was truly a great human being.

AGELESS WONDER

Some people had this thing about Marv's age because he was 60 when he started and 72 when he retired. But it was never an issue with the players. He was blessed with great genes and kept himself in excellent shape, often jogging three, four miles a day and working out with the weights.

Other than when he first came back from prostate surgery, I never saw him lacking for energy. And his mind was always razor sharp. Nobody on our team was faster on his mental "feet" than Marv.

Whenever someone brought up the fact he was the oldest coach in the NFL, he'd tell them, "I'm old enough to know my limitations and young enough to exceed them." Those words still ring true.

When Marv returned to the Bills as the general manager at age 80 in early January 2006, the age thing came up again, and I just scoffed. I was 43 at the time, and I told reporters that I hoped that I could be as young as Marv is when I'm 50, let alone 80.

MARV THE DISCIPLINARIAN

Some criticized Marv for not being a taskmaster, and I thought that criticism wasn't fair. Marv might not have been a yeller and screamer and a control freak, but with him you knew who the boss was.

Marv had a group of guys—team leaders such as Jim Kelly, Kent Hull, Darryl Talley, Cornelius Bennett, and Bruce Smith—he would consult with on occasion to gauge the mood of the team. He rarely fined guys, but instead would consult the core group about a problem with so-and-so, and they would take care of the matter.

There was an early-season game in Miami in which we were getting our butts kicked, and to avoid injuries Marv pulled most of the starters. Bruce was angry and confronted Marv on the sideline because he believed we were conceding defeat by pulling the starters, and the television cameras caught it.

Marv addressed the issue after the game, and he made it clear that he wasn't going to tolerate insubordination. His speech went something like this: "If I pull you out, it's for a good reason, and don't ever think that the only way we can win is with you in there. We've got good players on our bench too that I might want to play. It's my call, and if I want you to play, you better damn well get in there and play, and if I want you out of the game, you get your ass off the field. It's an insult to your teammates and an insult to me when you tell me we can't win with these guys in the game. Screw you. We can win. We are not giving up just because we put backups in the game."

Everything was fine after that, and nobody confronted Marv on the sideline like that again.

MARV'S BEST LESSON

Oh yeah, there was one other thing Marv taught us—how to win. We went 123-78 for a .612 winning percentage during his reign. In his 11 full seasons, we made it to the play-offs eight times. Yes, he had a lot of talented players during his time in Buffalo, but there've been a lot of coaches who haven't known how to handle talent. Marv did, and that's why there's a bust of him in Canton.

WHO WAS THAT GUY?

When I was playing for Houston, I met Oilers owner Bud Adams once in a reception line. That was my only personal encounter with him. During my year and a half in Texas, he might have addressed the entire team twice. He never came into the locker room before or after games, and I didn't think anything of it. I just figured this was the way it was in the NFL: each team is a big organization that makes tons of money, and the owner doesn't have time to stop by and say hi to the players—especially to unknowns like me.

Bills owner Ralph Wilson was beloved by most of his players.
Photo courtesy of the Rochester Democrat and Chronicle

So I came to Buffalo midway through the 1986 season. We beat Pittsburgh in our first game and headed to New England to play the Patriots a few weeks later. I was sitting in the visitors' locker room in Foxboro, and this man in a nice suit and trench coat came up to me and shook my hand. He told me how happy he was to have me on the team and asked me to let him know if I needed anything.

I thanked him, and after he was gone, I went up to our trainer, Eddie "Abe" Abramoski, and asked him, "Who the heck was that?"

"You idiot," Abe replied, laughing. "That was Ralph Wilson, the owner of the team."

"No way," I said, thinking Abe might be pulling my leg. "The owner of the Bills comes in before games? I'm not used to that." But I got used to it over time, and like all of my teammates, I came to love the fact Ralph was so involved and so passionate about his team.

One of the things we all liked about Ralph was his easygoing nature. Although he owned the team and was a bazillionaire, there were no airs about him. He loved coming to practices and hanging out with the coaches and players. He truly became one of the guys. He'd give hugs and shake hands and tell stories and crack jokes. He loved catching passes from Jim. (Fortunately, Kelly was smart enough not to deliver any fastballs, or he would have broken the boss's fingers.)

One time, I was fielding punts in practice, and Ralph came out to take a look. He was going to try to catch one himself, but when he saw how high it traveled, he backed off.

We would hear through the grapevine that Ralph had quite a temper. We heard how he had gone at it with some of the guys in the front office, but he never really was that way with us. With us, he acted like our favorite uncle. He was a lot of fun to be around.

RALPH ROCKNE

Ralph had a million stories, and one of my favorites concerned the time in the early 1960s when friends encouraged him to go down to the locker room during halftime and give his struggling Bills a pep talk.

"We were trailing the New York Titans 21–7 in War Memorial Stadium, the Old Rockpile, and I gave them one of the most inspiring speeches you'll ever hear," Ralph recalled. "I was like Rockne at Notre Dame. Well, the final score wound up being 51–7, and somebody said to me afterward, 'Wilson, you talked to the wrong team. You should have gone down and talked to the Titans.' Needless to say, that was the last time I ever addressed my players during a game."

MORE RALPH

When asked if he had been inundated by ticket requests for the Bills' first Super Bowl, Ralph Wilson quipped, "Yes, I have. I've heard from a lot of relatives I didn't know I had."

"MILD-MANNERED" BILL

I don't know of any general manager in any sport who's ever been more vehemently supportive of his players than Bill Polian, and we loved him for it. Bill's temper was legendary. Just ask any agent, fan, or member of the media who criticized one of his

Bills coach Marv Levy (left) and general manager Bill Polian were a dynamic duo. *Photo courtesy of the Rochester Democrat and Chronicle*

players or coaches. Bill believed his team was his family, so if you attacked one of us, you were attacking him, and he wasn't going to stand for it.

When he got going, it was a sight to see. The veins in his neck would bulge, and his face would turn as red as his hair. He once told a Buffalo columnist that if he didn't like the way the Bills were doing things, he could get out of town. And there were times, during contract negotiations with agents, Bill actually got down into a stance to demonstrate a blocking or tackling technique. Knowing his disdain for those guys, I'm surprised Bill never pancaked one of them to the floor.

Interestingly, he never acted that way with us. I can't ever recall seeing him angry with a player. We admired his pugnacious defense of us, and that's why we would run through hoops for him, although that was never the reason he did it. That was just his nature.

A BILL OF GOODS

Bill Polian is to football teams what Frank Lloyd Wright was to buildings—a master architect. You look at the work he did constructing championship teams in Buffalo, Carolina, and now in Indianapolis, and it's easy to understand why he's won more NFL Executive of the Year awards than anyone else.

Bill climbed the rungs of the ladder the old-fashioned way. He went from being an unknown part-time scout to one of the game's most brilliant GMs by working his butt off and approaching his job with unparalleled passion and intelligence.

He's as good a judge of talent as anyone in the game, and that was evident in the way he helped build our Super Bowl teams of the early '90s. Bill proved to be not only a shrewd judge of playing talent but a shrewd judge of coaching and front office talent too. He's the guy who hired Marv Levy to replace Hank Bullough as coach, and he also brought aboard John Butler and A. J. Smith, each of whom went on to become top NFL executives themselves.

Bill played a pivotal role in signing Jim Kelly after the USFL folded in the summer of '87—not an easy task, because Jim already had shunned Buffalo once and had strongly lobbied to be traded to a more glamorous franchise. Bill and his staff also were responsible for the drafting of players such as Bruce Smith, Andre Reed, Thurman Thomas, Will Wolford, Shane Conlan, Don Beebe, Howard Ballard, Nate Odomes, Keith McKeller, Jeff Wright, Carlton Bailey, Phil Hansen, and Mark Pike. He also engineered the blockbuster trade for Cornelius Bennett and the free agent signings of guys like yours truly, along with Kent Hull, James Lofton, Mark Kelso, and Leonard Smith.

I believe his greatest acquisition, though, was Marv. Bill had gotten to know Marv from their USFL days, and they had the utmost respect for one another. He knew Marv was the ideal coach to handle a team featuring some sizable egos. He also was on the same page with Marv as far as identifying players and people who would help him build a winner.

In the NFL, relationships between GMs and coaches can become strained. Sometimes when teams have success, there will be petty battles over who deserves the credit and who should hold the power. That was never the case with Bill and Marv. They worked together as well as any GM-coach combination I've seen, and I think that sometimes gets overlooked when people cite reasons for our success over time.

A COMMITMENT TO WINNING

We clinched the division a couple of times with several regular-season games left to play, and whenever we did, Marv often would rest his starters, so they would be fresh for the postseason.

I remember one time after that had happened, our general manager, Bill Polian, came into a team meeting and told us, "I know a lot of you guys have individual incentives in your contracts based on playing time and other things. I just want you to know that you don't have to worry about missing out on those incentives. We're going to take care of those of you who are close to reaching them. So if you deserve the money, you'll get it."

Some GMs and owners might have tried to nickel-and-dime their players out of that money, but Bill and Ralph Wilson understood it was important for team morale to make a move like they did. This was before the days of the salary cap, so if Ralph wanted to write the check, he could. And, by golly, he usually did.

It just made us want to play that much harder for the organization because we believed the front office was concerned about us and committed to winning in the postseason.

BIG JOHN

Like Bill Polian, "Big John" Butler was one of those guys who started at the bottom and worked his way up the football ladder the hard way. After serving with the Marines during the Vietnam War, Big John played offensive line for the University of Illinois, but a knee injury cut his career short. He wanted to stay involved in the game, so he did a little coaching before landing a job as a scout with the old USFL. That's where he became associated with Marv Levy and Bill Polian. And shortly after hooking up with the Bills, Bill hired John.

It was a brilliant addition, because John was one of the best evaluators in the game. He had a keen eye for talent. We had some bountiful drafts during our glory years, and many of those were the result of the hard work and astuteness of John and our scouting staff.

After Bill left following our second Super Bowl, John was promoted to GM, and we didn't miss a beat. John definitely was a player's general manager. Although he was a huge man with a handshake that could turn your bones into sawdust, John always came across to me as a gentle giant. He was a jovial sort who loved to come into the locker room before and after practice and shoot the breeze with us.

John's biggest fault was his smoking habit. He'd go through several packs of cigarettes a day and eventually developed lung cancer. When I first heard the news that he had the disease, I told reporters that if anyone could beat it, John could, because the guys who played for him didn't believe cancer was powerful enough to kill him. He was one of the toughest men in a game full of tough men. Sadly, we were wrong.

Although John had left Buffalo a few years earlier to become general manager of the San Diego Chargers, his death was a big blow to all of us in the Bills organization. He had played an integral role in building our great teams. We all miss him.

2

JIM, THURMAN, BRUCE, AND THE REST OF THE GANG

UNSELFISH JIM

J im Kelly finished his career among the top 15 quarterbacks of all-time in touchdown passes, completion percentage, and yardage. And there's no doubt in my mind that his statistics would have been even more impressive had he been more selfish. But Jim really was all about winning, not numbers, and if that meant audibling out of a pass play, he would. In fact, I bet you he changed to a run more often than he changed to a pass during his career. Some star quarterbacks overly concerned about their individual records wouldn't have done that. Jim wasn't like that.

The other thing people forget when assessing Jim's career is the conditions under which he played. It's not easy being a

Jim Kelly remains the standard by which all Bills quarterbacks are measured.
Photo by Jamie Germano/Rochester Democrat and Chronicle

quarterback in a cold-weather city like Buffalo. There are games here in November and December where the wind and frigid temperatures wreak havoc with throwing the football. And it's not just the games that take their toll. A lot of times players practice outside, and quarterbacks have to put extra zip on the ball to make it cut through the gale-force winds. That's a lot of extra stress on your throwing arm and shoulder, and it adds up over time.

But Jim never used that as an alibi. He just went out and overcame the weather as if it were merely another opponent.

I think people have come to appreciate Jim's greatness as a quarterback even more with the passage of time. They focus more on what Jim did rather than what the Bills didn't do. Like Babe Ruth was to the Yankees and Michael Jordan was to the Bulls, Jim Kelly is to the Bills. He taught us how to win and, in the process, saved the franchise.

HELL HATH NO FURY LIKE A QUARTERBACK SPURNED

All that stuff about Jim being a quarterback with a linebacker's mentality was true.

During our first Super Bowl season (1990), we were playing the Arizona Cardinals in Buffalo on an absolutely miserable day. There was freezing rain and snow and winds that seared through you like razor blades.

Early in the game, Jim dropped back to pass, and then-Cardinal safety Leonard Smith, who would play for us later on, blitzed and slammed into Jim's jaw. The ball came loose, and Jim hit the ground as if he had been shot. One of their defensive linemen scooped up the fumble and began lumbering toward our end zone. His return was like one of those rugby scrums—a mass of humanity pushing and tugging while inching down the field. It finally came to a halt at our 10-yard line. The referees unpiled the bodies, and I'll be darned if Jim wasn't at the bottom of the pile with the lineman who had picked up the fumble.

I guarantee you, not a single, solitary quarterback from that era—especially none of the other guys from the famous QB Class of '83—would have gotten up and chased that lineman down and tried to tear the guy's head off because he was so ticked.

Another time, we were playing the Atlanta Falcons, and this big safety picked Jim off at their 2-yard line and began sprinting the other way down the sideline. Jim got an angle on him and tackled him right in front of our bench at around our 40. The instant Jim laid into him, you could hear the guy's leg snap. It was a gruesome sight and sound. It wasn't Jim's intent to hurt the guy. But he definitely was determined not to let him score.

KELLY'S AUTHORITY

Marv and Ted Marchibroda treated Jim Kelly as an ally more than a player. They realized that in order for us to succeed, Jim was going to have to be comfortable, which meant he needed to have a major say in our play-calling and personnel decisions. That's the way it's done with all the great quarterbacks. It's almost as if they are elevated a little bit into the ranks of the coaching staff. They become part of the inner circle. Jim could go up to Marv and Ted in private and say, "Listen, this receiver can't play. Get rid of him." Which meant Jim and the position coach really were the ones choosing the receiving corps.

Frankly, it made sense to give Jim expanded authority, just as it made sense for the Chicago Bulls to give Michael Jordan expanded authority. To Jim's credit, he didn't abuse his power; he didn't get drunk on it like great quarterbacks on other teams did. He wouldn't tell the coaches to cut somebody just because he had personality differences with him. Jim was fine with things as long as the guy could play and help us win.

CELEBRITY JIM

It was really tough for Jim his first few years in Buffalo. He was like a whale in a goldfish tank. At times he felt like he was suffocating.

There were those who didn't like it that Jim had spurned the Bills the first time around when, following the 1983 draft, he went to play for the Houston Gamblers in the United States Football League (USFL). And then, at the time the USFL was folding, Jim shot his mouth off about how he would rather play with a more glamorous team like the Raiders. Along the way, he dissed Buffalo on television and in national magazines, and that didn't play well at all in western New York.

Plus, Jim had the misfortune of coming here at a time when the team was really bad and the expectations unrealistically high. People anointed him the savior from the start. Heck, some fans unfurled a "Kelly Is God" banner at Jim's first game. They expected an immediate turnaround, not understanding that the supporting cast here was weak and that it would take time for Bill Polian to fill in the holes around Jim. They wanted wins right away, and when that didn't happen, they took it out on their highly paid and highly publicized superstar.

For a time, it was like Jim had a target on his back whenever he went out. People wanted to take shots at him, bring him down. I remember being at a charity picnic where Jim and some folks were having a friendly water balloon fight. He hit this one woman with a balloon and she started laughing, no big deal. The next day, she showed up and said she was going to sue Jim for some ridiculous amount—I think it was $2 million. What had happened was her brother-in-law had slapped her on the side of her head and then said the bruise was caused by Jim's water-balloon toss. Fortunately, the authorities realized this was an attempt at extortion and the case was thrown out.

I made public appearances with Jim, and I can honestly say that I wouldn't have wanted to trade places with him. The unprovoked stuff he had to put up with was unbelievable. People would come up to him and say things that would have touched off a full-scale brawl had they been said to you or me.

He was constantly dealing with predators who wanted to take his money, so he really had to keep his guard up early on. To his credit, he learned how to turn his back on a lot of things. But believe me, it wasn't easy.

Eventually, though, he won people over by making the Bills winners. The critics came to see Jim as one of their own—a hard-nosed, salt-of-the-earth, blue-collar icon. He became part of the Buffalo family. He still is and always will be.

THURMAN THOMAS

Thurman lived his life with a chip on his shoulder, and Marv was more than happy to keep supplying the wood. I believe some of Thurman's fire was a result of him not being taken higher in the 1988 draft. He had been a great player at

Oklahoma State—so good that he kept Barry Sanders on the bench as his backup for two years. But Thurman had suffered a knee injury in college, and although he was completely recovered, a lot of NFL scouts were skeptical about him, so he slid all the way to the middle of the second round. Their slight wound up being our huge gain. I believe Thurman had all those doubting Thomases in the back of his mind every time he touched the ball.

He wound up getting angry—and even.

The guy was an absolute warrior, and for a long period, the most productive running back and perhaps the most productive offensive player in the game.

Thurman didn't like it when people called him football's most complete back, but people weren't denigrating him when they said that; they were paying him a high compliment.

The thing about Thurman was that, like Walter Payton before him, he was able to do it all, and do it all very well. He was a superb runner, rushing for more yards during his Buffalo career than O. J. Simpson. And he was an excellent receiver. Even die-hard fans might not know that Thurman ranks third all-time among Bills receivers with 456 receptions, 22 of them for touchdowns.

But his blocking skills were the thing that impressed me the most and spoke legions about what a team player he was. Thurman was one of the best backs in NFL history at picking up blitzers. I don't know how many times he waylaid a linebacker or a cornerback to give Jim the additional time to complete a big pass.

Thurman Thomas picks up yardage against the Patriots.
Photo by Jamie Germano/Rochester Democrat and Chronicle

That was no small thing, because most marquee backs want nothing to do with blocking. But Ted Marchibroda told me that Thurman would spend extra time during the week studying the blitz tendencies of upcoming opponents.

Four times, Thurman led the league in combined yards from scrimmage. He and the immortal Jim Brown are the only backs in league history to accomplish that feat that many times.

Thurman clearly was a dominating player over a long period. I think the voters who didn't put him in the Hall of Fame on the first ballot need to have their heads examined, because Thurman definitely belongs.

BRUCE SMITH

Bruce Smith was the best player at his position for a long stretch of his career, and there were times when he was the best player at any position in football. His ability to rush the passer from defensive end was unparalleled. It was almost unfair for a guy that big (6 feet, 4 inches, 275 pounds) and strong to have that kind of quickness and athleticism. His first step was unreal, and he was such a good athlete that he could pivot on a dime. He could blow by you, or spin by you or bowl you over. He had it all.

I remember one game against the Dolphins, Bruce shifted inside and lined directly over Miami's Hall of Fame center, Dwight Stephenson. Dwight had this "You've got to be kidding me" look on his face. Dan Marino was in a shotgun and called for the snap, and Dwight was so concerned about going one on one with Bruce that he rolled the ball back to Marino. And Dwight was no slouch of a player. But it just showed you the kind of havoc Bruce could wreak.

When other teams were making up their game plans, the first thing they attempted to account for was Bruce, because they knew how disruptive he was.

One time, Art Shell, one of the greatest offensive linemen in the history of the game, was asked how he would have handled Bruce if he were playing against him. Art, who was in his first stint as coach of the Oakland Raiders, said, "I'd beg for help. All you can do with a guy like that is try and stay in front of him and hope the quarterback gets rid of the damn ball in a hurry."

Anthony Munoz, another all-time great blocker, had a similar take, only, unlike Shell, he had an opportunity to get to know Bruce up close and personal. Before one of our games against the Cincinnati Bengals, Munoz was asked about facing Bruce, and he said simply, "It's scary."

As the NFL's all-time sack leader, Bruce is best known for bagging quarterbacks. But I don't think he gets enough credit for how well he played on first and second downs. He really became a force against the run. He was so strong, he could toss aside 300-pounders and pancake a running back. No wonder he made it to the Pro Bowl a team-record 11 times and was twice named the league's defensive player of the year.

Despite his enormous talent, Bruce wasn't always the easiest guy to coach. He definitely was high maintenance. He was kind of like your crazy uncle, but he was loved by his teammates. And he knew how to take a joke. We liked to razz him pretty good whenever he started singing. We'd be out there stretching, and he'd start singing some song. He'd have the lyrics all screwed up, and we wouldn't let him hear the end of it.

And Bruce liked to dance. Early in his career, he became pretty creative with his celebrations after making a sack. He had

Thurman Thomas and Bruce Smith (sunglasses) were two of the biggest stars during the Bills' unprecedented Super Bowl run.
Photo courtesy of the Rochester Democrat and Chronicle

his Fred Sanford "heart attack" routine and his PeeWee Herman dance. We got a kick out of them, unless, of course, we were getting our heads caved in. In those cases, his mentor and friend, Darryl Talley, usually would set Bruce straight.

ANDRE REED

When I first joined the Bills midway through that '86 season, Andre Reed was still a work in progress. You could tell right off the bat that he had tons of talent, but he was really raw. He ran his patterns hard, but they weren't real precise or disciplined.

The next season—Marv Levy's first full one as Bills head coach—I noticed a significant change in how Dre was running routes. You could tell that he had spent a lot of time in the off-season honing his skills. His improvement coincided with the changes that Ted Marchibroda was making in our offense—changes that included more throws to Dre.

The thing that struck me from day one was how strong he was. At 6 feet, 205 pounds, he didn't have the size of a prototypical NFL receiver. In fact, he was built more along the lines of a running back. But I think that served him well, because there have been few receivers in NFL history better at running patterns over the middle and gaining yards after the catch.

As time evolved, you could see Jim Kelly gaining more and more confidence in Dre. Jim connected with some very good receivers in Buffalo—guys like Hall of Famer James Lofton and speedster Don Beebe—but there's no question Dre was his favorite target, the guy he trusted most, especially in crunch time.

Of course, it took a little time for that trust to develop. But when it did, Dre wanted the ball even more. And if he didn't get it as much as he wanted it, he would pout. That isn't meant as a knock on Dre, but rather a compliment. All the great receivers are like that. They can't help it. Wanting the ball in their hands as much as possible is part of what makes them great. Jim fully understood this, and that's why he often would try to establish Dre early in games.

Bills all-time receiving great Andre Reed exceeded all expectations after being drafted out of tiny Kutztown University of Pennsylvania in the fourth round.
Photo courtesy of the Rochester Democrat and Chronicle

During his illustrious Bills career, the fourth-round pick from tiny Kutztown University in Pennsylvania established team records for receptions (941), receiving yards (13,095), and touchdown receptions (86) in a career. I don't think any Bill is ever going to break those marks.

Until Peyton Manning and Marvin Harrison did their thing, Jim and Dre were the most prolific passing combination in NFL history. There's no question in my mind that Dre, along with Jim, Marv, Thurman, and Bruce, was as much a part of our success as anybody during our glory years. He was a guy you had to game plan for.

Dre was one of several small-college diamonds in the rough unearthed by our crack scouting department. Interestingly, the guy who lobbied hardest for the Bills to draft Dre was former Buffalo receiving great, Elbert Dubenion, the man known as Golden Wheels because he could flat-out fly. He was a scout for Buffalo in the mid-1980s, and he immediately saw something in Dre that convinced him he would become a great player at the next level.

One other interesting tidbit about Dre. He played quarterback in high school and switched to receiver in college. I think being a former QB definitely helped him as a receiver, because he had a better understanding about what a signal-caller was looking for from a pass-catcher.

There's no doubt in my mind that Andre belongs in the Hall of Fame. Jerry Rice was the only receiver during that era more prolific than Dre. I think that's all you need to know.

KENT HULL

Kent Hull reported for his first training camp practice as a Bill on the same day that Jim Kelly did. Needless to say, the fans, players, and media were too busy fawning over Jim's first day in a Buffalo uniform to notice Kent. "Jim showed up in a stretch limo and [with a] police escort, while I arrived in Fredonia on the back of an equipment truck," Kent joked.

Though his signing didn't receive the franchise savior treatment that Jim's did, Kent's acquisition proved to be another brilliant move by Bill Polian. Bill had worked in the United States Football League before coming to the Bills, so he was familiar with the guys in that league who had NFL talent. Many teams were reluctant to take a chance on Kent, because he was considered a little too light and had come from a run-oriented program in college. But Bill saw something in Kent that others didn't, and Kent wound up becoming the greatest center in Bills history and one of the main components of our no-huddle attack.

He became the quarterback of our offensive line, so to speak, and also one of the smartest and most respected guys in the locker room. When he spoke in that thick-as-Mississippi-mud drawl of his, guys listened.

Simply put, the no-huddle would not have worked had we not had Kent at center. He was brilliant at quickly diagnosing defensive fronts and making blocking calls that put us in matchups that would enable a play to succeed. It wasn't an easy job, because our offense often operated at a breakneck pace. When we were really clicking, there were only about 16 seconds—real time, not play-clock time—between plays. So, Kent had to make snap decisions before snapping the ball, and if he screwed up, the play would blow up. He was so intelligent, there were times when he would look back and have Jim alter a play call. Jim trusted him implicitly.

I don't know whether this is true, but Kent claims he actually called a few plays for Jim after Jim suffered a concussion in Super Bowl XXVI against the Redskins. In fact, Kent said he called just the plays that resulted in scores for us, so it sounds a little fishy to me.

There was nothing fishy, though, about his intelligence on and off the field. The apple apparently didn't fall far from the tree. His dad had been the head of Mississippi's Department of Agriculture, and Kent eventually became a cattle rancher and farmer, too.

I think guys respected him not only for his brains and toughness but also for his honesty and humility. He wasn't afraid to point a finger at himself and say he had screwed up, and neither was he afraid to call out someone who wasn't doing his job.

Kent had a folksy, down-home perspective on things. He was always a stand-up guy. Win or lose, he'd be willing to talk to the reporters after a game, and I think that's one of the reasons the guys in the media liked him so much. In fact, they liked him so much that after he announced his retirement, they took him out to Illio DiPaolo's for lunch and presented him with a newspaper page that contained tributes from each of the beat reporters and columnists who covered the team. That is unheard of, but it speaks volumes about what kind of guy Kent was.

THE HIT MAN

Linebacker Shane Conlan may have boasted one of the most disproportionate bodies I've ever seen on a football player. He had a huge head, a huge torso, and legs skinnier than a pelican's. Guys in the locker room would joke that the Buffalo Jills cheerleaders had more meat on their gams than Shane did.

But those toothpick legs didn't prevent Conlan from delivering some of the most hellacious hits you'd ever want to see. He was your classic run-stuffing linebacker. He had kind of an old-school style. He would have fit in nicely with guys like Butkus and Nitschke.

There was one time against the Jets that he pancaked Roger Vick so hard that we thought he was dead. Kent Hull said after the game, "I was looking for a priest to give the guy his last rites."

DON BEEBE

I've known few players more resilient than my long-time teammate and good friend, Don Beebe. He was like those old Timex watches that would take a licking but keep on ticking.

Beebs suffered a major concussion his rookie season. The next year, he broke his leg in two places. His third year, he snapped his collarbone. That's why, going into his fourth season, I joked with him that his goal should be to make it through 16 games in one piece.

Fortunately, Beebs stuck with it and became a dynamic part of our offense as a wide receiver. He had freakish speed and was able to scare the dickens out of defensive backs. His ability to stretch defenses opened things up for fellow pass-catchers Andre

Don Beebe, wearing a helment with an extra protective shell to prevent concussions, makes a catch during a loss to the Minnesota Vikings.
Photo by Jamie Germano/Rochester Democrat and Chronicle

Reed, James Lofton, Keith McKeller, Pete Metzelaars, and me. Plus, he prevented opposing teams from stacking eight men in the box and ganging up on Thurman Thomas and our run game.

Beebs' greatest performance came in a 1991 game against Pittsburgh when he hauled in four touchdown receptions in a 52–34 blowout at Rich Stadium. No one was more pleased with that performance than Jim Kelly, who grew up in Western Pennsylvania and badly wanted to beat the team he rooted for as a boy.

Beebs wound up having a productive nine-year NFL career as a third receiver for the Bills, Carolina Panthers, and Green Bay Packers. He caught 219 passes for 3,416 yards and 23 touchdowns and earned that elusive Super Bowl ring while playing with Brett Favre and the Pack.

Not bad for a third-round draft pick out of tiny Chadron State in Nebraska.

BRUCE DeHAVEN

I know I'm biased, but I think one of the big reasons for our success during our Super Bowl run was the play of our special teams. And the man behind that success was Bruce DeHaven. His game plans were always right on. He's the reason we were annually among the league leaders in kickoff and punt coverage, and the reason we were able to block so many punts and field-goal attempts. He always had us prepared. We once awarded him a game ball—not for the work he had done that day, but rather for the work he had done the six days leading up to the game.

It may have seemed like Bruce was in a tough spot, because his boss, Marv Levy, had broken into the NFL as a special teams coach, and it remained Marv's area of expertise. But Bruce never acted as if it were a burden, as if someone were looking over his shoulder waiting to micromanage things. Bruce was secure enough in his ability to use Marv as an advisor, sounding board, and confidante. He knew he had one of the all-time great special teams guys at his disposal and took advantage of him as a mentor.

Marv was always there for our unit meetings and would sit in the front row. But not once in my time with the Bills did I ever hear Marv contradict anything Bruce said. The only time he ever interrupted was to reinforce some point Bruce was trying to drive home.

Bruce also realized that having Marv as his boss meant special teams would never get shortchanged. Marv realized the importance of the kicking game long before other NFL head coaches. Kickoffs, punts, and placekicks accounted for nearly a third of the plays, so Marv felt it was imperative we emphasize special teams nearly as much as we did offense and defense.

I think Bruce had one of the greatest demeanors of any coach ever. I never heard him raise his voice or hang anyone out to dry. He was one of the most positive guys I've ever been around. He started out as my position coach but wound up becoming a really good friend of mine. He still is.

DARRYL TALLEY

I played with and against a lot of tough guys in the NFL, but nobody had a higher pain threshold than Darryl Talley. He was like the Black Knight in Monty Python and the Holy Grail;

even with his arms and legs cut off, he would still want to fight you. He'd be out there with broken bones and torn muscles and strained ligaments, and you wouldn't hear a peep from the guy. You could count on him every Sunday.

I'd be on the sideline, watching him play at his usual high level, and our trainer, Eddie Abramoski, would come up to me and say, "I can't believe Darryl's even in uniform today." When Abe said something like that, you took heed, because nobody had a better read on tough Bills through the years than he.

Everybody—and I mean everybody—on the team respected Darryl, and they feared him too. Nobody wanted to mess with him. He clearly was one of our leaders, and he was not afraid to speak his piece when he believed it was necessary. He'd tell Bruce Smith to shut up and sit down, and he'd pull Jim aside and say, "Jim, you can't do that. You've got to knock it off." And Jim and Bruce and all the other stars would listen to him and take his words to heart.

Darryl was a positive influence on Bruce. He would counsel Bruce on matters about football and life. I think he played a huge role in Bruce realizing his potential as a Hall of Fame–caliber player.

Darryl was a lot of fun to be around, in the locker room and out on the town. He could drink any three sailors under the table.

No one loved Buffalo and Bills fans more than Darryl. When he left the team as a Plan B free agency casualty following the 1994 season, he took out a full-page ad in the *Buffalo News* thanking the fans of Western New York. That was Darryl—a class act.

ABE

One of my all-time favorite Bills was our trainer, Eddie Abramoski. Abe had been with the team almost as long as Ralph Wilson had, so he had pretty much seen it all as far as pro football was concerned. He was a guy you could confide in, a guy whose advice you always sought. Abe was quite the character. Guys liked to bust his chops about his prodigious appetite and waistline, and his hobbies, which included racing homing pigeons. And Abe would give it right back to guys, good-naturedly.

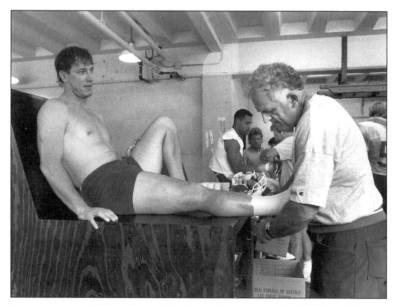

Longtime trainer Eddie Abramoski, shown here taping Jim Kelly's ankle, was beloved by players and coaches alike. *Photo courtesy of the Rochester Democrat and Chronicle*

Unless you didn't care about giving away money, there were two things in which you didn't try to compete against Abe: card games and chicken wing–eating contests. He'd crush you in both.

Abe made a seamless transition from the days when trainers treated everything with ice and tape to the modern era of MRIs and cybex machines.

I had a bunch of injuries during my career, and Abe was always right on the money with the diagnosis and the type of rehab I needed. He'd grab your leg, say you had a pulled hammy, and tell you how long it would take to get back to full speed.

Abe knew the difference between pain and injury. He'd tell you, "If you want to go, you can without risking further injury, but it's up to you." And he'd also be firm in making sure you didn't play when you shouldn't be playing. He knew the line between toughness and stupidity.

FRED SMERLAS

I spent parts of four seasons as Fred's teammate, and I wish I could have played more years with him, because our mountainous, mustachioed nose tackle was a great player and quite the entertainer. A little kid definitely resided in that big man's body.

The first paragraph of his autobiography, *By a Nose*, gives you great insight into his mischievous nature.

"I make a living as a nose tackle," Fred wrote with the help of sportswriter Vic Carucci. "This should tell you right away there are a few loose toys in my attic. No one in his right mind would spend more than a single play there. I've been in my wrong mind for 11 years. There isn't another player in league history who has spent more time at that position. I guess that makes me a nose for the ages."

Fred was an immovable object up-front—an incredibly powerful 300-pounder who would tie up blockers so others could make tackles. He made it to the Pro Bowl five times doing the grunt work on the defensive line that often goes overlooked. Centers hated seeing him lined across from them.

Fred had a great sense of humor and a stadium full of strong opinions. He loved to hold court in the locker room. Politics, religion, football, clothing—anything was fair game.

Like many linemen, Fred was sort of a slob. To say his locker was a pigsty would be an insult to pigs. He had more shoes than Imelda Marcos piled in there, along with balled-up junk food wrappers and who knows what else.

We once had a problem with mice in the locker room, and they had to bring exterminators in there to get rid of them. Legend has it that they even didn't bother with Fred's locker because it was so filthy even a mouse wouldn't take up residency there.

HARDLY OVER THE HILL

We added another big piece of the puzzle on September 26, 1989, when Bill Polian signed James Lofton as a free agent. A lot of people thought the seven-time Pro Bowl receiver was washed up, but Polian, thanks to some heavy prodding by our receivers coach, Nick Nicolau, believed that James still had some good football left in him.

Burly Bills nose tackle Fred Smerlas gets to New England Patriots quarterback Doug Flutie. *Photo by Jamie Germano/Rochester Democrat and Chronicle*

While with the Green Bay Packers and Oakland Raiders, James had been given one of the all-time great nicknames. Teammates and opponents alike referred to him simply as "The Bomb" because of his ability to leave defensive backs in the dust.

We quickly discovered that The Bomb still was plenty explosive. His ability to stretch a defense gave Andre Reed more room to operate because teams couldn't double him as much. James helped Andre and the rest of us receivers with the mental part of the game. He was a consummate professional who had seen it all as far as pass coverages were concerned, and he was able to pass along his knowledge to the rest of us.

After he finished playing, James went on to coach receivers in college and the NFL. He interviewed for the Bills' vacant head coaching job in 2006, and although he didn't land it, there's no doubt in my mind that he one day will be running a pro football team. He's just so bright, so professional, and so good with people. James has always been one of those classy guys who walks into a room and immediately commands your respect.

PETE METZELAARS

It's hard to believe that a guy who's 6-foot-8 could be overshadowed, but Pete Metzelaars definitely was. In fact, our sequoia-sized tight end might have been the most overlooked and least appreciated player from our Super Bowl years. Part of it had to do with our abundance of stars on offense. When you have guys like Jim Kelly, Thurman Thomas, Andre Reed, and James Lofton doing their thing, it's hard not to get lost in the

Pete Metzelaars, shown here celebrating one of the 25 touchdowns he scored during his Bills career, played more games at tight end than any player in NFL history. *Photo by Jamie Germano/Rochester Democrat and Chronicle*

shuffle. Plus, we had another talented tight end in Keith McKeller—the guy whom our K-Gun personnel grouping was named after.

But Pete played a valuable role for us. He was our Kellen Winslow without the breakaway speed. People probably don't realize this, but Pete played more games at tight end than anyone in NFL history—226 to be exact. And, believe you me, you don't hang around for that many games unless you're something special. Pete's longevity is attributable to three things he could do very well: pass block, run block, and catch anything thrown his way.

One time we went up against Denver and their great pass-rushing defensive end, Simon Fletcher. Our game plan called for Pete to pass block most of the day, and he wound up shutting down Fletcher cold.

Pete had been a superb basketball player at Wabash College. He was so good that he led his team to a small-college national championship and earned the nickname "The Wabash Cannonball." Pete's basketball background helped make him a sure-handed pass-catcher. Jim Kelly knew that if he were in trouble, he could always count on dependable Pete to bail him out with a reception.

The only thing Pete really lacked was a fifth gear. Or maybe even a fourth-gear for that matter. After he caught the ball, he lumbered rather than ran. But he was so sound at all other phases of the game that it didn't matter. And he was such a sound blocker that some of us thought Pete might put on 20 pounds toward the end of his career and line up as an offensive tackle. If he had, he'd still be playing in his 28th year in the league.

HOUSE BALLARD

At 6 feet, 6 inches, and well over 300 pounds, Howard "House" Ballard was one of the largest human beings I've ever seen on or off a football field—a veritable walking solar eclipse. The interesting thing about our gigantic right tackle is that it took a couple of years before he saw the field for us. He was considered a "project" back in the pre–free agency days, when you could afford to keep projects on your roster. The Bills picked him out of Alabama A&M in the 11th round of the 1987 NFL Draft, and he wound up becoming one of several late-round picks from small schools who became big contributors to our success.

Howard was a hard guy not to like, a soft-spoken, gentle giant with a big heart. A few games into his first season as a starter in 1989, Howard found himself in the news when he missed a block that resulted in Jim being sacked and injured. Jim was seething after the game and hung Howard out to dry. Howard didn't let the comments bother him. He realized that Jim said them in the heat of the moment and just let them slide. Jim later apologized to House, and House said no apology was necessary.

Howard wound up becoming a Pro Bowl player for us. Unfortunately, when free agency came along, we couldn't afford to keep him. It was a big loss for us, literally and figuratively.

During his years with us, Howard spent his off-seasons back in Alabama working in law enforcement. After retiring, he became a sheriff's deputy. If I were a criminal, the last thing I would want to do is go one on one with Officer Ballard.

TED MARCHIBRODA

Perhaps Marv's best coaching hire was Ted Marchibroda as our offensive coordinator. Ted had worked with some excellent quarterbacks through the years, guys like Sonny Jerguson, Ron Jaworski, and Bert Jones. His vast football knowledge and fatherly approach helped Jim Kelly realize his Hall of Fame potential.

Ted was a master at fitting the offense to the quarterback rather than the other way around. Over time, he realized that Jim's skills were best suited for the fast-paced, no-huddle attack that became our calling card. Jim respected the fact Ted trusted him enough to allow him to call his own plays on the field. And Jim proved he was worthy of that trust. All he cared about was getting us into a play that had the greatest chance of succeeding, and if that meant handing the ball off more often than throwing it, Jim was all for that.

Ted had been a successful head coach with the old Baltimore Colts, but his most notable football feat may have occurred early during his brief NFL playing career. Ted had lettered in football for St. Bonaventure University in the 1950s and wound up being drafted by the Pittsburgh Steelers. During his first training camp, Ted beat out the great Johnny Unitas for a roster spot. Unitas, of course, signed with the Colts and went on to become the greatest quarterback in the history of the game in the minds of many football experts.

Another interesting tidbit about Ted: when he was with the Colts, he gave a 23-year-old by the name of Bill Belichick his start in coaching. In an interesting twist, Belichick was the

Giants' defensive coordinator in Super Bowl XXV, years before he became a household name as the head coach of the New England Patriots dynasty.

DARBY THE LINEBACKER

Ray Bentley was a big fan of Alice Cooper, so in honor of the rock legend, Ray started painting the musician's infamous black teardrops on his face before every football game. The teardrops along with Ray's Fu Manchu mustache gave him a menacing appearance—not a bad image to project when you are a linebacker.

Off the field, Ray was a lot of fun. He loved pranks. His best one may have been when he nailed Fred Smerlas' cleats to the locker room floor before practice.

Ray was a really bright guy. He developed the Darby the Dinosaur cartoon character, and along with our teammate, Mike Hamby, who was a gifted illustrator, published a series of children's books that became popular in Western New York. Ray later went on to do network announcing as both a color guy and a play-by-play guy and spent some time coaching in the Arena Football League.

MARK PIKE

I was blessed to go to the Pro Bowl seven times, but in reality, my teammate, Mark Pike, should have gone in my place at least a few times.

Marv Levy called Mark "the best big-man special teams player" he ever saw, and I would second that motion. At 6 feet, 4 inches, and 272 pounds, Mark was hardly your normal kick

Ray Bentley was a ferocious linebacker on the field, but a sensitive children's author away from it. *Photo courtesy of the Rochester Democrat and Chronicle*

and punt cover guy. But he had excellent quickness and speed for his size, and he was a very sure tackler. Kick returners often felt they had been squashed by a tank when they were hit by Mark.

Mark and I complemented each other extremely well. He often knocked out a few blockers, enabling me to knife my way through for the tackle. And when teams started double-teaming me, Mark usually was there to flatten the kick or punt returner.

A backup defensive end, Mark played 193 games for the Bills—and 192 of his starts came on special teams. He actually finished his career with more tackles than I did. They say timing is everything, and that certainly was true for him and me. The fact we played in Buffalo when Marv was there enabled each of us to have long, productive careers as special teamers.

KELSO THE SAVIOR

One time when we were flying back from a Monday night game, we went through some pretty rough turbulence. I mean, the plane was bouncing around so much that even some of the big, tough guys were getting nervous and sick. In the middle of all this, Mitch Frerotte, a big offensive lineman and one of our crazier dudes, got up and started running frantically up and down the aisle. He finally found where our safety Mark Kelso was sitting and plopped himself down right next do him. We asked him why he did that, and he said, "If this plane goes down, I know one guy God is going to save, and I want to be sitting next to him."

That may sound strange, but that's the way everybody on the team felt about Mark. He was as well-grounded and as big-hearted as anybody I've ever met. I never heard anybody say a bad word about him. We tried to bust his chops for being such a straight arrow, but we could never get a rise out of him.

Mark is now the radio analyst for the Bills—which means people can hear for themselves what a good guy Mark truly is.

JOE DEVLIN

Joe Devlin was one of the best offensive tackles in football and probably the most intimidating guy I ever played with. He was big—280 pounds of lean muscle on a 6-foot-5 frame—and he was mean.

Joe was tight with guys like Freddy Smerlas and some of the older offensive linemen, but he had no use for wide receivers, defensive backs, or kickers. So, when you saw him in the locker room, you'd take a real wide route to avoid him, like you would if you were in the presence of a bear.

When I joined the Bills, older veterans like Joe and Freddy were the team leaders. Those were the days when leadership was based on seniority. But around that time, the NFL's locker-room hierarchy was beginning to change. Some began according leadership to the star players rather than the most senior players.

When Bills management let Joe and Freddy go following the 1989 season, the leadership void was filled by Jim and Bruce, because they were the biggest and highest-paid stars as well as our best players. It's like that on most teams today. That's not to say that others can't be team leaders. Guys like Darryl Talley and Kent Hull clearly were respected and listened to on our team, but they didn't quite have the clout that Jim or Bruce or Thurman had.

Getting back to Joe—I always felt it was a shame he never made it to a Pro Bowl. This was a guy who used to own great pass-rushers such as Mark Gastineau, but for some reason opponents never gave him the accolades he deserved. Perhaps it was because he spent so much of his career playing on losing teams.

WALT COREY

Walt Corey, our swizzle stick–chewing defensive coordinator, was an old-school football coach. He had been a solid linebacker for the Kansas City Chiefs during their Super Bowl years, and he came from an era when there were just 33 roster spots and you had to fear for your job.

He believed the defensive side of the ball was more about emotions than brains, so he would rip guys in order to get them mad and motivate them. I remember him coming in at halftime on more than one occasion and curse his defense like a longshoreman. He'd blister them up one side and down the other. "Forget about adjustments," he'd bellow. "We are going to go back out there and play a base defense in the second half, and you had better play a lot better, or there's going to be hell to pay next week."

It was totally opposite of the scientific, cerebral approach taken by our offensive coordinator, Teddy Marchibroda, but it usually worked. We had some very talented players on defense, and they usually responded to Walt's halftime harangues. Despite the occasional outbursts, most of the guys really liked and respected Walt, because he had played the game at a high level. I also believe they liked the fact that he didn't try to gunk things up with complicated read-and-react schemes. He liked turning guys loose, and people like Bruce and Cornelius really appreciated that.

JIM RICHTER

Jim Richter was one of those guys I would expect to find in those "World's Strongest Man" competitions. He wasn't all that tall for an offensive lineman, maybe 6 feet, 2 inches and change, and he had problems keeping his weight above 280, but you didn't want to mess with him because he was so incredibly strong.

Freddie Smerlas, who was considerably heavier and as strong as an ox himself, credits Richter with helping him become a Pro Bowl nose tackle. Early in his career, Jim played center, and he and Freddie would lock horns every day in practice. That had to be like watching two 18-wheelers going head to head.

It was funny seeing rookies line up for pass-rushing drills the first day of training camp. They'd choose to go up against Richter because he appeared to be the smallest offensive lineman, and they figured they could have their way with him. They quickly discovered otherwise. More times than not, Richter wound up manhandling them.

Freddie told me there was a time when a rookie started a fight with Richter after Jim cleaned his clock in a one-on-one drill. Richter grabbed the guy by his facemask and twisted him to the ground like he was a pretzel.

Jim always had a fascination with flying, and in the off-season he earned his pilot's license. During several of our charter flights, Jim would be allowed in the cockpit. When he stopped playing football, Jim realized his dream by becoming a pilot for American Airlines. These days, the guy who used to teach rookie defensive linemen a lesson and open holes for Thurman Thomas, spends his time flying coast to coast.

JOHN KIDD

My move from Houston to Buffalo would have been more difficult if it weren't for John Kidd. We had been teammates at Northwestern, and when I was acquired by the Bills midway through the 1986 season, John and his wife, Heidi, invited me to live with them until Sarah arrived three weeks later.

Like most players in the NFL, John had been an exceptional athlete in high school. He had been recruited to play quarterback in college and was such an outstanding hockey player in the Detroit area that there was talk about his NHL potential.

But John wound up making his mark as a punter, and believe me there were few better. His rookie year with the Bills, he led the league in net yardage and set a record for most punts inside the 20-yard line. This, mind you, while competing with the frigid temperatures and swirling gusts of Rich Stadium. I've known John for more than half of my life, and he remains one of my closest friends.

STEVE CHRISTIE

Nothing against Scott Norwood, but his accuracy plummeted the season following his infamous missed field goal in Super Bowl XXV, and you could sense that it was time for him and the Bills to part ways.

In another shrewd and brilliant move by Bill Polian, we signed Steve Christie to a free agent contract. Though he had been kicking in the comfy climes of Tampa, Christie had no problems adjusting to the cold, windy conditions of Orchard Park. In fact, Steve went on to become not only the Bills' all-time leading scorer but also one of the great clutch kickers in the history of the game. There had to have been at least 15 occasions on which Steve came on and nailed the winning field goal in the waning minutes of a game.

As our special teams coach Bruce DeHaven once said about him, "The more the kick means, the better he kicks. He makes all of us look good."

Steve converted 80 percent of his field goals during his Bills career, and he established the team record not only for accuracy but also for distance with a 59-yarder. When he was in his prime, I saw him boot some field goals in practice that were close to 70 yards. He had a cannon for a leg.

3

CROSSING THE RIVER TO TAMPA AND OTHER SUPER MOMENTS

BILLS 51, RAIDERS 3

Before we headed out of the Rich Stadium tunnel to play the Raiders in the AFC championship game following the 1990 season, Marv Levy sang "One More River." I love Marv, but singing isn't his forte. One of my teammates put it best when he said, "As a singer, Marv is one hell of a football coach."

That said, the symbolism of the song Marv chose wasn't lost on us. There was one more river to cross to reach our goal of playing in our first Super Bowl, and the big, bad Raiders were the team intent on stopping us from making it to Tampa.

During that regular season, we had staged a furious fourth-quarter comeback to beat the Silver and Black in Orchard Park, and afterward some of their players groused about us being lucky. But like Branch Rickey, the sage Brooklyn Dodgers general manager, once said, "Luck is the residue of design." In other words, we had worked very hard to make our breaks, and coming into that title game, I could sense that we were supremely prepared to make a statement.

Still, I never expected to make a statement quite as loud as the one we did.

Emotions ran extremely high at Rich Stadium that day. The Persian Gulf military effort was just days away from starting, and you could feel the patriotic fervor in the stands. One of my teammates, Carlton Bailey, was especially fired up. His dad was one of our soldiers stationed in Saudi Arabia, and Carlton knew his dad and other American soldiers would be watching the game on a special telecast to our troops.

As the band from West Point played the national anthem, many of us grew a little misty-eyed thinking about Carlton's dad and all the other brave men and women preparing for Operation Desert Storm. When the playing of "The Star-Spangled Banner" concluded, the majority of the spectators in the crowd of 80,324 broke into a chants of "U-S-A! U-S-A! U-S-A!"

I couldn't help but notice all the American flags in the stands. In fact, after the game, I told a reporter that the best banner of the day wasn't "Just Lose Baby," or "Who Cares What Bo (Jackson) Knows," but rather the Stars and Stripes.

As Marv had reminded us, we had one more river to cross, and we wound up using the backs of the Raiders as our bridge.

Simply put, we turned in the most complete and dominating performance in the Bills' storied history, scoring 41 points in the first half en route to a 51–3 annihilation.

The tone was set shortly after we received the opening kickoff as Jim Kelly went 75 yards in nine plays and capped the drive with a 19-yard touchdown pass to future Hall of Fame receiver James Lofton. We moved the ball so effortlessly and so quickly that the Raiders actually had to call a time-out about six plays into the drive to regroup.

To their credit, the Raiders came right back and kicked a field goal, but that was merely the calm before the storm. Jim answered that by taking us 66 yards in just four plays, and the march culminated in a 12-yard touchdown run by Thurman Thomas on a draw. Then Darryl Talley intercepted Jay Schroeder and sprinted 27 yards for a score that put us up 21–3.

The Raiders tried all sorts of defenses against us that day— six defensive backs, all-out blitzes—but nothing worked. We were unstoppable.

Kenny Davis scored on short touchdown runs on our next two possessions—the first of those scores was set up by yours truly when I hauled in a 44-yard pass from Jim along the sideline.

The second half was somewhat surreal, because we knew we had the game in hand. The Raiders undoubtedly wished they didn't have to come out for the second half. I remember toward the end, seeing fans holding up huge letters spelling out the word *Tampa*, the site of Super Bowl XXV.

THE VINDICATION OF DARRYL TALLEY

As you might imagine, the locker room was crazy after that game, and perhaps no one was happier than Darryl. I felt so happy for him because he had endured the 2-14 seasons and all those cruel jokes.

One that he related to reporters went like this:

"Knock, knock."

"Who's there?"

"Owen."

"Owen who?"

"Oh-and-10."

Darryl was arguably the most respected guy in our locker room—a consummate professional who had seen it all and wasn't afraid to stand up to the superstars if he felt it was necessary.

He wound up having a monster game at outside linebacker that day, intercepting two passes and batting down another.

For some reason, Darryl was always overlooked in Pro Bowl balloting, but on that day, he just might have been the best player on a field filled with stars. Fittingly, a few days later, while we were in Tampa prepping for the Super Bowl, the announcement came that Raiders coach Art Shell had added Darryl to the AFC Pro Bowl squad. It was an honor well deserved and long overdue.

THE BIRTH OF THE NO-HUDDLE

We certainly had a tumultuous season in 1989, but everything happens for a reason, and out of the tumult we

Linebacker Darryl Talley may have had the highest pain threshold of any Bill.
Photo by Jamie Germano/Rochester Democrat and Chronicle

wound up discovering the no-huddle offense that became our calling card. It was born during a disappointing but exciting 34–30 AFC wild-card playoff loss to the Browns at dilapidated Cleveland Stadium.

We fell behind in that game and were forced to run our two-minute, hurry-up offense for much of the second half. And Jim Kelly ran it to absolute perfection, throwing for more than 400 yards—a figure that could have easily been 500 yards had we not dropped so many catchable passes, including one by Ronnie Harmon in the end zone that would have won the game for us.

During that off-season, Jim lobbied hard for us to go to that offense full-time. His rationale in his meetings with Marv Levy and offensive coordinator Ted Marchibroda was simple but right on: "If it works, why would you do anything else? If they can't stop us, don't let *us* stop us. Let me do it, and let's see if they can stop us."

Marv and Ted figured Jim was on to something and said, "Why not?"

In the first game of the 1990 season, we sprung it on the Colts, and they didn't know what had hit them. We went down that field like a hot knife through butter. Boom. Boom. Boom. Boom. Boom. Touchdown.

Other teams had run no-huddles before, but never with the amount of success we had. I think we had the perfect ingredients: a smart, well-conditioned offensive line; solid tight ends; a wide receiving corps that featured future Hall of Famers James Lofton and Andre Reed; the league's most prolific yardage producer four years running in Thurman Thomas; and a quarterback who always managed to get the football in the hands of the player who could do the most damage on any given play.

When it hummed the way it did during the early 1990s, our no-huddle was virtually unstoppable, and Jim operated it with the dead-on efficiency of Magic Johnson running a fast break in his basketball prime.

We set a franchise record with 428 points in 16 games that first season. That total probably would have been over 500 if we hadn't gotten out to such huge leads in so many of our games, prompting us to call the dogs off and substitute freely by the fourth quarter.

The beauty of our offense was that it forced opposing defenses to be simple because there was no time for situational substitutions, and it took the starch out of the pass rush. Our offense was geared to run a play every 16 seconds—I'm talking real time, not game time—and by the time we were into the fifth or sixth play of the drive, those 320-pound defensive linemen were sucking wind big time. There would be drives when defenders had to call a timeout literally just to catch their breath.

We dictated the pace of the game and forced defenses to react to us rather than the other way around. It seemed like we always took the lead first during that 1990 season, and that put a lot of pressure on the other team, because they always had to answer us right off the bat. In fact, in the 12 games leading up to Super Bowl XXV, we scored on our first possession 10 times, and nine of those scores were touchdowns.

Will Wolford was one of the mainstays of an offensive line that paved the way to four consecutive Super Bowl appearances.
Photo by Jamie Germano/Rochester Democrat and Chronicle

Jim really loved the pedal-to-the-metal attack because it gave him the opportunity to call his own plays—making him a rarity among modern-day quarterbacks. Peyton Manning is the only current quarterback who has similar authority.

If Jim was the star of the no-huddle, center Kent Hull was its unsung hero. Besides identifying defensive formations and making the appropriate calls for the offensive line, Kent also would shake off certain calls Jim might make. It was kind of like a catcher advising a pitcher about what he should throw. I remember several occasions when Jim would call a play at the line, and Kent would turn his head around and give him this "you can't run this play, you idiot" look, and Jim would change the call.

A lot of people perceive the no-huddle to be a pass-happy offense. But we actually had great balance between the run and pass during our Super Bowl years. There were more occasions than not when Jim would change the play from a pass to a run after examining the defensive formation. And it was a great offense to run out of because we were able to spread defenses out and create natural holes that our offensive line would exploit. It's no coincidence that Thurman managed eight consecutive 1,000-yard rushing seasons in his years with the Bills.

One last thing about our no-huddle: it was called the K-Gun, and a lot of people think it was named for Kelly. But in reality, K-Gun stood for the personnel grouping that involved our tight end, Keith McKeller. Keith was kind of a mix between a tight end and a wide receiver. He was a guy who could run a downfield pattern, so with him out there, it was essentially like having four wideouts, which put even more stress on defenses.

IN DEFENSE OF THE DEFENSE

A lot of prognosticators made us the preseason favorites to repeat as AFC champs and go on to win Super Bowl XXVI, and the foundation for those predictions was our offense.

The No-Huddle was really humming during the 1991 season as we established club records for points (458), yards (6,252), and wins (13). Nine times that year, we scored 30 or more points, and Jim Kelly led the league in touchdown passes while Thurman Thomas led the league in most yards gained from scrimmage. Even Bill Walsh, who achieved genius status while guiding the San Francisco 49ers of Joe Montana and Jerry Rice to three Super Bowl titles, was impressed. He called us unstoppable after seeing us destroy an opponent early in the season and said we had a chance to become the greatest offense of all-time.

Our defense, meanwhile, wasn't receiving much pub. Despite the presence of star performers such as Bruce Smith, Cornelius Bennett, and Darryl Talley, we had given up more yards that season than all but one team. That is why when Denver came to town for the AFC championship game on January 12, 1992, most people were figuring the game would be a shoot-out between Kelly and John Elway.

But that's what's great about this game: you just never know what's going to happen. And on that day, to the surprise of the experts, defense ruled. The Broncos wound up picking Jim off twice, and our offense mustered just 213 yards—a figure we were used to racking up in a quarter and change.

Elway wasn't much better, thanks to a stout effort by our much-maligned defense. Thanks to a tipped pass by our nose tackle, Jeff Wright, that resulted in an 11-yard interception return for a touchdown by linebacker Carlton Bailey, we were able to escape with a 10–7 victory and earn our second trip to the Super Bowl.

The decisive play came on a middle screen that Jeff read perfectly. The Broncos had had success with the call a few times earlier in the game, but this time, Jeff diagnosed it right away, and instead of boring in on Elway, Jeff dropped back toward the intended receiver and wound up deflecting the pass. We were quite fortunate that Carlton held onto the ball, because he didn't have the greatest hands in the world. In fact, guys were always razzing him in practice because he kept dropping interceptions.

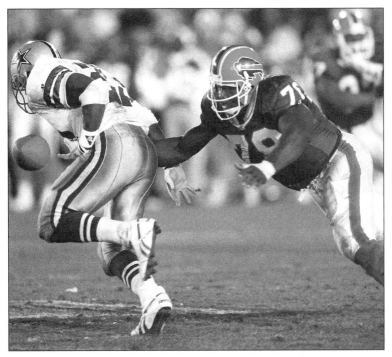

Bruce Smith, shown here making a tackle in the Super Bowl, gave opposing quarterbacks nightmares. *Photo by Jamie Germano/Rochester Democrat and Chronicle*

After the game, our defense reveled in its performance—as well it should have.

Jeff told reporters, "Defense wins championships, and we were a big part of it today. The offense carried us all season; we just paid them back."

THURMAN TAKES A STANCE

I think one of the turning points for us came early during the 1989 season, the year we became known as the "Bickering Bills." In week 5, we went to Indianapolis to play the Colts, and we wound up getting our asses handed to us. Adding injury to insult, Jim Kelly wound up suffering a separated shoulder while being sacked.

Jim was understandably angry and frustrated, and after the game he blamed offensive tackle Howard Ballard. In the heat of the moment, he told the media that if House hadn't fanned on his block, he wouldn't have been sacked and injured, which may have been true, but when you are a quarterback and a team leader, you don't publicly blast your guys.

Needless to say, the you-know-what hit the fan after Jim mouthed off. The fans and media ripped him big time, and deservedly so. The funny thing is that Howard didn't seem to take the public criticism badly at all. He just sloughed it off as Jim saying something in a moment of frustration.

But the rest of us knew Jim shouldn't have pointed the finger at Howard to the media. No one was more upset than Thurman Thomas. He stood up to Jim and told him that he was wrong to call out House. He said, "Listen here, Jim. You're not the only guy out there trying. You make your share of mistakes too. We all do, and we need to realize that if we want to be a good team."

Thurman was only in his second year as a pro. He hadn't yet achieved league MVP status, so it took courage for him to do what he did. He earned an awful lot of respect from his teammates.

Later that season, when Jim was struggling, Thurman reopened the can of worms when he appeared on the Paul Maguire Show and said that "quarterback was a position that needed upgrading." The media picked up on it, and the Bills public relations staff had another fire to fight.

Two days later, in one of the all-time great press conferences in Bills history, Jim and Thurman appeared together in front of reporters and read prepared statements that essentially said, "We win as a team and lose as a team." It was very awkward, because it was staged, but I think it was something the management needed Jim and Thurman to do in order to put this fire out once and for all.

I believe Thurman's stance really began to open up the lines of communication in our locker room. Guys actually started having honest conversations with one another, and the dialogue led to the friendships and the bonds that helped make us into champions.

If Thurman had done that in a place like Miami, where Dan Marino was king, or San Diego with Dan Fouts at quarterback, I guarantee he would have been traded. Those quarterbacks would not have allowed any second-year guy to question their authority.

Thurman Thomas, being interviewed at the Super Bowl, wasn't afraid to speak his piece. *Photo by Jamie Germano/Rochester Democrat and Chronicle*

But to Jim's credit, he didn't storm into Bill Polian's office and demand he jettison Thurman. Instead, he took what Thurman said to heart and realized his mistake.

I think we all learned a valuable lesson from that incident. Thanks to Thurman and Jim, a situation that easily could have torn our team asunder wound up drawing us closer.

ANOTHER WEEK WOULD HAVE BEEN GREAT

When I look back at that shellacking of the Raiders in the AFC championship game, I regret that we didn't have a two-week break before Super Bowl XXV. Because of the way the NFL schedule was set up that year, only one week separated the two games, which meant we had to go home and pack and hop on the charter for Tampa the next morning. It would have been so cool if we could have stayed in Buffalo for a week and basked in the euphoria we felt from thrashing the Raiders. But we really never had a chance to do that, and neither did our fans. It really made the whole experience feel like a blur. The celebration wound up being short because there was a game to prepare for—the biggest one of our lives.

A BIG HALLOWEEN TREAT

One of the biggest trades in football history—and certainly the biggest in Bills annals—occurred on Halloween night, 1987.

We wound up getting Cornelius "Biscuit" Bennett from the Indianapolis Colts in exchange for running back Greg Bell and two future first-round draft picks. The Colts, in turn, dealt Bell and the draft picks to the Los Angeles Rams in exchange for running back Eric Dickerson. At the time, some thought we had paid too much for the gifted-but-untested linebacker from the University of Alabama, but my teammates and I thought our general manager, Bill Polian, had gotten away with highway robbery.

It was at that point that all the guys in our locker room began to look at Polian differently. We began to realize that this guy was a genius—and certainly not somebody you wanted to play poker against, because Bill was as shrewd as they came about knowing when to hold 'em and knowing when to fold 'em.

Biscuit had been the top pick of the Colts, but he had held out the entire first half of the season in a contract dispute, so

Indy was only too happy to cut its losses and get something in return. And we were only too happy to part ways with Bell, who some of the veterans regarded as a prima donna.

It didn't take long for Biscuit to make a contribution. In fact, on his very first play in the pros—just a week after he arrived in Buffalo—Biscuit flushed John Elway out of the pocket and batted down his pass. We were all like, "Wow! Did you see that?" It was an incredibly athletic play, because Elway was the most mobile quarterback in the league at the time—a guy who could hurt you as much with his legs as his arm.

Biscuit had a sack, two quarterback pressures, and three tackles in limited action that day. It wound up being a sneak preview of what would become a smashing Bills career. He totally transformed our defense. With him out there, offenses could no longer focus so much of their attention on stopping Bruce Smith. Teams were forced to pick their poison: "Do we put an extra blocker on Bruce or on Bennett?"

They were both sensational pass rushers, and over time, they developed a friendly competition to see who would get more sacks. Bruce usually finished with more, but I recall a couple of occasions on which they both arrived at the quarterback at the same time from opposite ends and were awarded half-sacks. I felt sorry for the poor QB in those situations. It couldn't be too much fun being sandwiched simultaneously by a 275-pound guy on one side and a 250-pound guy on the other.

Through the years, I saw Biscuit turn in many sensational performances, but perhaps his best occurred in our 1987 season finale against the Eagles in Philadelphia's Veterans Stadium. Biscuit, in what may have been the most dominating defensive

Linebacker Cornelius Bennett, shown here helping up Denver quarterback John Elway, made an immediate impact on the Bills defense.

Photo by Jamie Germano/Rochester Democrat and Chronicle

performance ever by a Bill, made 16 tackles, had four sacks for a total of 34 lost yards, and forced three fumbles. He was just unblockable that day.

Trades are best judged after several seasons, and history shows us that by far we got the better of the deal. Yes, Dickerson was a Hall of Fame running back, but he was on the downside of his career by the time he arrived in Indianapolis. None of the draft picks we parted with wound up doing anything with the Rams, and although Bell turned in a 1,000-yard season with the Rams, we wound up drafting Thurman Thomas in the second round in '88, and all he did was put together a Hall of Fame–caliber career.

Bill clearly has made a number of shrewd deals during his illustrious career as a general manager, but I believe the trade for Biscuit was his most brilliant.

ENDING THE DIVISIONAL DROUGHT

One of the most breathtaking and frightening sights I've ever witnessed at a football game occurred after we beat the New Jets 9–6 in overtime at Rich Stadium to win the AFC East title on November 20, 1988. Fred Smerlas blocked a Pat Leahy chip-shot field goal near the end of regulation that would have won it for the Jets, and Scott Norwood connected in the extra session to give us our 11th victory in 12 games. It was one of four or five game-winners that Scottie booted for us that season—a fact that often gets overlooked by people who fixate on Wide Right.

That win was a stepping-stone victory for us, and marked a remarkable turnaround for a franchise that had won just six of its previous 41 games before Marv replaced Hank Bullough as coach just a season and a half earlier.

We knew Bills fans would be ecstatic with their first divisional title in seven years, but nothing prepared us for the scene that unfolded the instant Scottie's kick sailed between the uprights. It was as if a dam burst as people flooded out of the stands and onto the field. I was no fool. I decided to get behind the mountainous Smerlas and follow his lead blocking through the sea of crazies to the locker room. But things were so chaotic that even Freddie got knocked over at one point, and believe me, that's not an easy thing to do.

We eventually made it to the safety of the tunnel, and for several minutes we watched the riotous celebration in awe and fear. There was an eerie feel to the scene. Fog was rising from the thousands of people who had gathered on the field. It looked as if someone had dropped a giant smoke bomb out there.

I remember both sets of goalposts being toppled. Fans passed one of the uprights through the stands and up to Mr. Wilson's luxury box. Ralph was in his glory. I'm told that a piece of one of the uprights from that game now resides in the ESPN office of star announcer and staunch Bills supporter Chris Berman in Bristol, Connecticut. I was happy to see our fans so happy, but I also was afraid that someone might get crushed to death out there.

That January, we hosted Houston in a second-round playoff game—the first postseason game in Buffalo in 23 years—and Polian brought in mounted policemen. But that didn't stop another field-storming celebration. The horses wound up becoming skittish, and the policemen had their hands full just getting the scared animals off the field.

The third time, Bill got it right. He brought in police dogs. A show of the canines' teeth was enough to convince the fans to stay in the stands.

HOME COOKING

There was a stretch there in the early 1990s when we felt invincible at home. We won a club-record 17 consecutive games at Rich Stadium, and it would have stretched even further had Marv not made the correct decision and rested most of our starters for our regular-season home-finale in 1991. An inferior Detroit Lions team wound up beating our second-stringers 17–14 in overtime. There's no doubt in my mind had we played our starters the entire game, we would have beaten the Lions handily.

But we were 13-2 at the time and had already clinched the AFC East as well as home field advantage throughout the playoffs, so Marv didn't want to risk injury to any key players in a meaningless game.

Thurman was a little ticked at first when he learned he wouldn't play much, because he had a chance to win the NFL rushing title. Plus, he was looking forward to going head-to-head with his former Oklahoma State teammate, Barry Sanders, who was tearing it up for Detroit.

But Marv explained to him that the team goal of winning the Super Bowl was more important than the individual goal of winning a rushing title, and Thurman understood that.

Our ability to dominate at home was a key component in our Super Bowl run. Commentators liked to say that the road to the Super Bowl would go through Buffalo, and they were right. We figured if we won our division and posted the best record in the conference, our chances of reaching the big game were pretty good. Only once did we fail to hold serve, so to speak, and that was during the 1992 season, when we had to win road playoff games in Pittsburgh and Miami in order to reach Super Bowl XXVII.

4

IT AIN'T OVER TILL IT'S OVER

A COMEBACK FOR THE AGES

People remember where they were when JFK was shot or when man first landed on the moon. Well, in our part of the country, people will never forget where they were on January 3, 1993. That was the day when the Bills wiped out a 32-point second-half deficit to beat the Oilers in the biggest, most improbable comeback in NFL history.

That wild-card playoff victory continues to be ingrained in the consciousness of Western New Yorkers all these years later. Rarely a week goes by when someone doesn't bring it up to me, and, unlike our Super Bowls, that is one game I never tire of reminiscing about.

It's probably bigger in Buffalo than the Ice Bowl is in Green Bay or the Immaculate Reception is in Pittsburgh, because those cities have experienced eight Super Bowl victories between them. Since the Bills haven't won any, we kind of hang our hats on that comeback game. Looking back, I think it really sums up the resiliency and the never-say-die attitude of our teams from the late 1980s, early '90s. In a way, it was our crowning moment.

I think Marv Levy captured the magnitude of what we had accomplished in that 41–38 overtime victory during his postgame news conference. A reporter asked him what the odds were of coming back from such a huge deficit, and Marv answered, "About the same as winning the New York State Lottery," more than a million to one.

The headline in the *Buffalo News* the day following the game summed it up beautifully. It read simply "UN-BILL-IEVABLE."

Some of my friends in the media told me they were writing obituaries for our season in the press box by halftime. I couldn't blame them, because I was feeling the same way. In fact, as we jogged up the tunnel to our locker room during halftime, the majority of us wanted to join the thousands of fans who had left Rich Stadium early. The Oilers were humiliating us 28–3 by that time, and the last thing we wanted to do was go out and play two more quarters.

I remember Marv kept his remarks brief during halftime. All he said was, "Don't ever let 'em say you gave up." There was brilliance in his simplicity. He didn't berate us for crappy play, and he didn't try to give us some rah-rah speech, which would have come across as disingenuous and phony. We had been to two straight Super Bowls, and he appealed to our pride. It wound up working. We chipped away and kept playing hard, and a miracle occurred.

Marv had a knack for always finding the right thing to say. He wasn't a believer in Knute Rockne, "Win one for the Gipper" speeches. He didn't like ripping us. But what he said had an effect on us, one way or another. It either got us mad at our opponents or mad at ourselves. Marv was a master psychologist at knowing what buttons to push.

Fortunately for us, Frank Reich, the quarterback who engineered the comeback, never stopped believing. He was playing in place of Jim Kelly, who was injured the week before, and as we took the field for the second half, Jim and our third-string quarterback, Gale Gilbert, reminded Frank about how Frank had authored the greatest comeback in college football history while at Maryland. "Maybe lightning will strike twice," Jim told him.

I guess Jim's encouraging words didn't work right away, because Frank tossed an interception on our first series of the third quarter that Bubba McDowell returned for a touchdown to put us down 35–3.

To his credit, Frank remained unfazed. He kept saying we had to play the game one down at a time. We all thought he was crazy, but he was taking the right approach. There's no such thing as a 32-point play. You have to chip away a little at a time and catch a few breaks, which we did.

Frank's career will always be defined by that game, and I couldn't be happier, because he is one of the finest people I've ever met, in or out of football. We couldn't have staged the comeback without him. He never lost his cool, and that was the way he always was: unflappable. He told reporters that other than getting married and having kids, the comeback against the Oilers was the greatest day of his life. He was not alone in that feeling.

What made that comeback all the more remarkable is that we did it without three of our biggest studs. Jim and Cornelius Bennett were out with injuries, and Thurman Thomas was knocked out of the game early on.

One interesting side note to that game is that it was blacked out throughout Western New York, so the only people who saw it live were the 75,141 fans who showed up at the stadium.

We closed the gap to 35–17 on a 38-yard touchdown pass from Frank to Don Beebe. It's funny, but we caught a big break on the play because Beebs ran out of bounds and came back in, which means he should have been declared an ineligible receiver, negating the score. But the officials didn't see it, so the infraction went uncalled.

Despite the break, I still didn't think we were going to win. I just thought, "Well, at least now we won't get blown out and look like total idiots." Then we scored again. And again. In what seemed like the blink of an eye, we went from trying to preserve our dignity to trying to look respectable to trying to win. It seemed like one supernatural thing after another kept happening.

We definitely got lucky, but I also believe the Oilers, after jumping out to such a huge lead, had turned the afterburners off and couldn't get them back on.

I remember looking into the stands in the third quarter and seeing so many empty seats. But when we made the comeback, people were literally climbing the fences to get back in.

Thanks to two second-half TD passes from Frank to Andre Reed, we took a 38–35 lead late in the game.

The Oilers, though, behind quarterback Warren Moon, weren't through. As regulation time wound down, Moon, who had a superb first half, drove Houston to our 12-yard line. But the Oilers were unable to punch it in, and Al Del Greco came on to kick a 26-yard field goal with 12 seconds to go to tie the game and send it into overtime.

Houston then won the coin toss, and I thought to myself how cruel it would be to come back this far and then lose.

Fortunately, cornerback Nate Odomes intercepted a pass on the Oilers' first possession, and Steve Christie won the game with a 32-yard field goal. It was Steve's first postseason appearance, and I remember him saying afterward, "Wow! Are all playoff games like this?"

Our locker room was a madhouse after that game. Guys were singing and jumping up and down. It was surreal.

Everywhere I go, I run into people who claim they were there that day. If they are all telling the truth, our attendance should have been about a quarter of a million.

I'm told the visiting locker room was like a funeral home. Their guys looked as if they had just been run over by a locomotive. The game became legendary in Houston, but for a different reason.

Oilers cornerback Cris Dishman summed up his team's collapse in a postgame interview. "It was the biggest choke job in history," he told reporters. "Everyone on the team, everyone in the organization, choked. We were outplayed and outcoached in the second half. When we had them down, we should have cut their throats, but we let them breathe and gave them new life. Never in my wildest nightmares did I believe something like this could happen. I think we have to put another word in the English dictionary to describe this loss because *devastated* doesn't do it. Tell me I'm dreaming and this didn't happen."

I'll never forget being in our training room the day after our miraculous comeback. A couple of the guys and I were still euphoric, still trying to get our minds around what had happened 24 hours earlier, and in walked Marv. He listened for a few seconds and then said with a straight face, "Hey, did you guys catch the end of that game yesterday? I left at halftime."

We burst out laughing.

THE REICH STUFF

Frank Reich made believers of us all long before that famous comeback game. His legacy as the perfect fill-in quarterback actually began with another comeback he engineered for us during a Monday-night game against the Los Angeles Rams on October 16, 1989.

Frank had thrown a total of just 41 passes in regular-season games up to that point and was forced into action the week after Jim suffered a separated shoulder in a loss to Indianapolis. Most of the fans and the media were forecasting doom for us. They said our season was about to go down the tubes because Kelly was to be sidelined for at least three weeks. But we had faith in Frank. We felt he was prepared.

He got off to a shaky start but settled down in the second half and was brilliant in the fourth quarter, when he brought us back from deficits twice to spark us to a 23–20 win with an 8-yard touchdown toss to Andre Reed with 16 seconds left. Frank went 7-for-7 on that final drive, and was 10-for-11 on our last two drives.

Frank Reich (No. 14) proved to be a valuable backup to Jim Kelly.
Photo by Jamie Germano/Rochester Democrat and Chronicle

There were several other occasions during our run when Frank came to the rescue, most notably during the playoffs following the 1992 season, when he engineered victories against Houston at home and Pittsburgh on the road before turning the reins back over to Jim.

I think Frank's greatest value, though, may have been as a quasi–assistant quarterbacks coach. Frank was an extremely bright guy, and Jim trusted him implicitly. Frank was like an extra set of eyes for Jim, and when Jim came to the sideline, Frank would point out things the defense was doing and suggest plays that might be successful. I think he played a huge role in Jim's development as a quarterback.

Everybody on the team really respected Frank. He was a quiet, big-hearted person who was deeply religious. There is no question his strong faith in God helped him keep his bearings during difficult times. He was and is now a great example of how I wish I could live my life.

IN THE BLINK OF AN EYE

During our Super Bowl years, our offense developed a reputation—and deservedly so—for putting points up on the board in a hurry. But the greatest scoring binge in Bills and perhaps NFL history, wound up being manufactured by our defense and special teams during a September 30, 1990, game against John Elway and the Denver Broncos.

In the span of just 77 seconds, we scored 20 points to turn a 12-point deficit into an eight-point lead. If my math's right that's a point every 3.9 seconds.

For the first three quarters and change, the Broncos had absolutely manhandled us. I mean, they were so dominating, they should have been up by 20 to 30 points.

But sometimes, like a boxer who's getting the crap kicked out of him for 14 rounds, you have to try to hold on until you can spring that knockout punch.

Leading by 12 early in the fourth quarter, Denver's David Treadwell lined up for a field goal. Nate Odomes roared in and blocked it, and Cornelius Bennett picked up the loose ball and raced 80 yards for a touchdown that cut the deficit to 21–16.

Cornelius Bennett returns a blocked kick for a touchdown against New England. *Photo by Jamie Germano/Rochester Democrat and Chronicle*

On the Broncos' second play of their next series, defensive end Leon Seals deflected Elway's pass, and Leonard Smith picked it off and sprinted 39 yards to make it 22–21. Scott Norwood hit the upright with his extra-point attempt, so our lead stood at just one point—but not for long.

Elway fumbled away the snap on Denver's first play from scrimmage following Scott's miss, and Biscuit recovered at the 2. Kenny Davis then scored to make it 29–21 with nine minutes to go. To their credit, the Broncos made things interesting, scoring once more, and we had to hang on for dear life to secure a 29–28 victory.

FOURTH-QUARTER FURY

A week after that 20-point explosion in just 77 seconds against Denver, we saved our best for last again, scoring 24 points in the fourth quarter to come from behind and beat the Raiders 38–24.

With a little more than seven minutes remaining in the game, the Raiders seemed in complete control. They had pushed us around pretty good and were holding a 10-point lead when Jeff Gossett went back to punt. JD Williams zoomed in untouched, forcing Gossett to move in the opposite direction to get off the punt. But he wound up turning right into me, and I blocked his kick. JD scooped up the football and ran 38 yards for the touchdown that closed the gap to three points.

On Los Angeles' next possession, Cornelius Bennett sacked Jay Schroeder, forcing a fumble to set up Scott Norwood's game-tying 23-yard field goal.

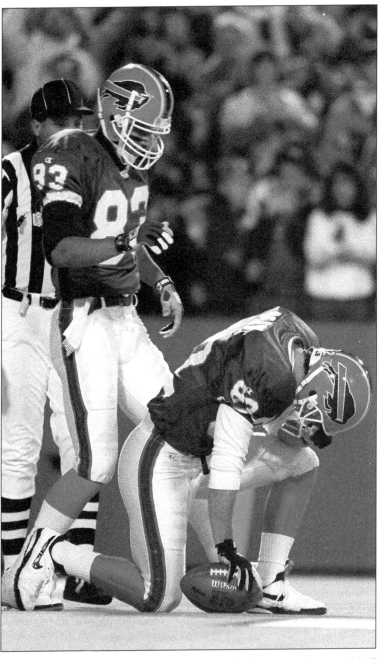

Don Beebe prays with fellow wideout Andre Reed after scoring during a 35-7 victory against Houston in 1993. *Photo by Jamie Germano/Rochester Democrat and Chronicle*

Then, on the Raiders' ensuing series, Nate Odomes literally stole the ball from the hands of LA receiver Willie Gault and ran it in for the go-ahead score.

The 80,076 fans in Rich Stadium had to have been wondering whether they were watching a replay of the game the week before. Like Yogi Berra would say, it was déjà vu all over again.

The 24-point outburst was the biggest fourth-quarter output in team history and reinforced our belief that we were never out of it.

DONNIE HUSTLE

Although he will be remembered for enduring several concussions and broken bones resulting from hellacious, *SportsCenter*-highlight hits, the most memorable play in Don Beebe's productive Bills career will always be the one in which he chased down Leon Lett in Super Bowl XXVII.

We were well on our way to that embarrassing 52–17 loss to the Dallas Cowboys that miserable evening in Pasadena, when Lett picked up a Frank Reich fumble at about their 30 and began rumbling down the field like a locomotive. Just before the big defensive end reached the end zone, he started slowing down and celebrating. It was a huge mistake because it gave Don time to catch him from behind and pop the ball out of his hands.

It was a great hustle play—Beebs had been out on a pass pattern on the play, so he had to sprint nearly the length of the field to catch him. But we didn't think much of it at the time, because any of us would have tried to chase Lett down in that situation. Plus, we were too ticked off about the way we had played to feel good about anything that night.

But all Don's teammates and coaches—along with countless others not associated with the Bills—have come to appreciate the magnitude of the play with the passage of time. It came to symbolize our team's refusal to give up, even under dire circumstances, and remains the high point of those four Super Bowls.

Nearly a decade later, Don still hears about that play when he's out in public.

I do too. I swear, every few weeks somebody asks me what it felt like to run Leon Lett down. I tell them, "I wouldn't know, but Don Beebe would." I give Beebs grief about it every time it happens. I did promise him that I wouldn't take credit for it.

The April following the play, he received bundles of mail. Among the items was this really cool putter with a head made out of flat river stone. There was an accompanying thank-you note in which the gift-giver explained how he had won a Super Bowl pool as a result of Beebs' hustle play and that the prize was so huge he was able to start his own golf club company.

That was pretty cool.

5

WIDE RIGHT, A MISSING HELMET, AND OTHER LAMENTABLE MOMENTS

FOUR REASONS

Whenever I hear the expression "wide right," I can't help but think of Scott Norwood. I feel so badly for Scottie. Even though I know he has things in perspective, it's a shame that so many people associate him primarily with the field goal he missed in Super Bowl XXV.

Kickers have it tough. I could miss a tackle on a kickoff or punt return and one of 10 other guys could cover up my mistake for me by bringing down the ballcarrier. But with a kicker, it is an all-or-nothing proposition. It's either good or no-good, hit or miss.

There are several things people forget when it comes to Scottie.

First, that Super Bowl against the Giants never should have come down to a last-second field-goal attempt. Everybody on our team—me included—deserves blame. Each of us could have done something a little bit better that might have swayed the outcome in our favor.

Second, even though I felt we were the better team, the Giants simply outplayed us that day. Bill Parcells knew there was only one way to shut down our high-powered offense, and that was by keeping Jim Kelly and Co. off the field. Their offensive line and running back Ottis Anderson did a brilliant job of controlling the clock, as evidenced by their 41–19 advantage in minutes of possession.

Third, although a 47-yard field goal is makeable, it is by no means a chip-shot. And further, Scottie had never made one from that distance on a grass surface.

And fourth, Scottie played an integral role during our rise from basement dwellers to penthouse residents. He made a lot of clutch kicks along the way. In 1988, when we turned the corner and went 12-4 to win the division, Scottie converted four game-winning field goals. He wound up going to the Pro Bowl after that season. He remains the only kicker in Bills history to earn a trip to Hawaii.

SCOTT'S CHARACTER

One of the things I'll always admire about Scottie is the way he answered reporters' questions after what's become known in Buffalo as "The Miss." He stayed at his locker for nearly an hour, responding to the same painful questions. I don't know if I could have been that gracious after my dream turned into a nightmare. I wouldn't have blamed him if he had blown people

Sadly, Scott Norwood is remembered more for his missed field goal in Super Bowl XXV than the numerous clutch kicks he made during his Bills career.
Photo by Jamie Germano/Rochester Democrat and Chronicle

off and had taken the first cab out of the stadium. But that was Scottie. He always was a stand-up guy. And I think the way he handled what amounted to an inquisition and blamed himself for the loss really resonated with people.

About a dozen of us were scheduled to play in the Pro Bowl in Hawaii, so we didn't get a chance to attend the rally held in

Niagara Square in downtown Buffalo the day after the loss. I'm told there were about 20,000 people on hand, and they began chanting: "We want Scott! We want Scott!" Overcome with emotion, he grabbed the mic and told the fans, "I know I've never felt more love than I do right now. We all realize the sun's going to come up tomorrow. I want to dedicate the 1991 season to Bills fans."

Before next training camp, he was inundated with thousands of letters and cards from all over the country. Some of them were from elementary school classes encouraging him to keep his head up. A lot of them were from coaches and parents who said Scottie had set a wonderful example of standing up and facing the music during the toughest of times.

It's funny, but I still run into people who think that that was the last kick Scottie ever attempted. They forget that he kicked for us the next season, including in Super Bowl XXVI in Minneapolis.

Yeah, I might think of Scottie whenever I hear the words *wide right*. And yeah, I wish that kick would have hooked a few feet to the left and been good. But I've never thought of Scottie as a loser. He was my teammate and my friend, and he should be remembered as much for all the clutch kicks he made as for the one he missed.

THANK GOODNESS HE MADE THAT KICK

In the season after The Miss, we played a bizarre game in Oakland in which Scott Norwood was not his usual, accurate self. He missed three makeable field goals and botched an extra point, sending a game we should have won in regulation into overtime. Scottie finally got it right the third time, booting a 42-yard field goal that enabled us to leave town with a 30–27 victory.

Following the game, Thurman Thomas told reporters, "If he missed that last one, we would have booted his butt off the plane over Denver without a parachute."

He was joking. At least, I think he was.

ANOTHER KICKER STORY

Speaking of kickers and missed field goals, our long-time trainer, Eddie Abramoski, had a great story about Booth Lusteg, who played for the Bills in mid-1960s. Lusteg botched a 23-yarder in the closing seconds against the San Diego Chargers at old War Memorial Stadium, and the game ended in a 17–17 tie. Apparently, on his way home from the stadium, which wasn't in the best of the neighborhoods, Lusteg was jumped and beaten up by a group of teenagers. When police later asked Lusteg why he hadn't called for help, he said, "Because I deserved it."

RAISING THE BAHR

Several years after Super Bowl XXV, I ran into Matt Bahr at Bills training camp. Matt had been the kicker for the Giants when they beat us in Tampa, and I immediately went up to him and told him, "You know Matt, Scott Norwood didn't lose that game for us; you won it for your team." I recounted how he had made two touchdown-saving tackles against us on kickoff returns.

He seemed pleasantly surprised that I had remembered his two overlooked plays. He said he felt badly for Scottie. Kickers are a close-knit fraternity, and Matt knew that there, but for the grace of God, went he. That having been said, however, you can bet the mortgage that when Scottie lined up for that kick in Super Bowl XXV, Matt, like the rest of the Giants, was pulling for our guy to miss.

Interestingly, the week before Matt had literally booted the Giants into the Super Bowl with five field goals—included the game winner from 42 yards—in a 15–13 victory against Joe Montana and the 49ers in San Francisco.

SOME EERIE WORDS BEFORE SUPER BOWL XXV

A sportswriter recently showed me some quotes he had gathered for stories the week leading up to Super Bowl XXV. One was from our Pro Bowl linebacker, Cornelius Bennett, the other from Pete Gogolak, a former kicker with both the Bills and Giants.

In retrospect, they are kind of spooky.

Bennett told the reporter, "I hope we win by a really big margin or lose by a really big margin. I don't want to lose it in the waning seconds of the game, because that would be awfully hard to swallow, to lose like that."

Asked for a prediction, Gogolak said, "All I'm going to say is it will be a close game. It will come down to a field goal."

Biscuit's worst fears—and mine—were realized, and Gogolak's words proved prophetic as the game came down to Scott Norwood's attempt in the final seconds.

SOMEBODY STILL LOVES ME

As you can imagine, the feeling in the locker room following that loss in Super Bowl XXV was one of utter despair and devastation. We had just climbed Mt. Everest that season, only to discover that we were at the bottom again. I remember Marv coming in after the game and telling us, "I know how you are feeling, guys. I feel the same way. But I'll tell you this: if I had to pick my team again, I'd still pick you guys—every last one of you." I remember thinking, "I'm glad somebody still loves me, because I don't think even my family likes me too much right now."

PROUD TO BE A PART OF IT

Patriotic feelings ran high at Super Bowl XXV, and when we took the field before the game, I couldn't help but notice the primary colors for both us and the Giants were, fittingly, red, white, and blue. The Persian Gulf War had just started, and we were told that our troops would be watching us from half a world away on Armed Forces television, so all of us wanted to put on a good show—especially my teammate, Carlton Bailey, whose dad was stationed over there.

Everybody who entered Tampa Stadium was given tiny American flags. There was a jet fighter flyover and huge Apache attack helicopters hovering above the stadium to protect the airspace. After Whitney Houston finished her rousing rendition of "The Star-Spangled Banner," 80,000 people began chanting in unison, "U-S-A! U-S-A! U-S-A!" I was crying, and so was just about everyone else. It was such an emotional moment, and I think both teams went out and put on a show that fans will talk about for as long as the Super Bowl exists. Even though we lost, I still consider that the greatest game I've ever been involved in. Not only because of what happened on the field, but because it was Buffalo's first Super Bowl and the Gulf War had just begun. For most of the guys on both teams, it was our first experience of dealing with our country being at war because we were too young to have any real memories of even the Vietnam War.

HAIL TO THE REDSKINS

Based solely on the scoreboard, many people would say that the best team we played in the Super Bowl was the Dallas Cowboys squad that clobbered us 52–17 in 1993. But I beg to differ. I think, of the four teams that beat us, the Washington Redskins were easily the best. They had a great offensive line that totally dominated us, and their defense, led by guys like Wilbur Marshall, smothered us.

Thurman, who was coming off a season in which he was named the league's MVP, managed just 13 yards on 10 carries, and Jim was sacked five times and intercepted four times.

Jim wound up suffering a concussion and doesn't remember much from that game. That's probably a good thing, because the memories from that contest in the Minneapolis Metrodome aren't pleasant.

BEEBE HIT IN PITTSBURGH

The Steelers were consistently the most physical team we played. There was just something about them. I think they took on the persona of their tough-guy coach, Bill Cowher, and their blue-collar fans.

There was one time we went down to Three Rivers Stadium for a Monday night game, and they just knocked the snot out of us. They harassed Jim Kelly the entire night, and he wound up committing two turnovers that they cashed in for scores. We got hammered 23–0, and interestingly, there wasn't a single touchdown by the offense in that game.

That was the night when Don Beebe got hit so hard his body looked like it was going to sail into the stands. It was a clean hit, but it was so sick that the referee threw a flag for unnecessary roughness. I'm sure the ref was thinking, "If this guy is going to die here, I should at least throw a penalty flag."

IN THIS CORNER, WEIGHING 175 POUNDS . . .

If you had to pick one incident that epitomized our Bickering Bills season, it was the fight between receivers coach Nick Nicolau and offensive line coach Tom Bresnahan. Talk about bizarre.

I remember sitting in the meeting room when in walked Bresnahan with this humongous bandage wrapped around his head. I mean, the thing was enormous. It looked like a turban. We were on a tight schedule that day, so none of us had a chance to ask him about it. We just figured he had gotten into a car accident or had taken a bad fall.

Once the team meeting ended, we split up into our unit meetings. The receivers and I hopped the elevator to our meeting on the top floor of the administration building at Rich Stadium, and when we walked into the room, we saw this huge, blood-stained hole in one of the walls. We asked Nick what the heck had happened, and he told us kind of sheepishly that he and Bresnahan had gotten into a fight earlier that morning. We were shocked.

"You're kidding," we said. "You drove Tom's head through that wall?" And, then we started to bust on him. "Way to go, Nick!"

What's amazing is that Nick was only about 5 feet, 10 inches, 190, and Tom was probably 6 feet, 4 inches, 260 pounds. But we also realized that Nick, a street-tough guy from a hardscrabble Philadelphia neighborhood, wasn't somebody you wanted to mess with, and this only confirmed it.

Years later, Nick told all of us what had prompted the fight. I guess Nick thought that Bresnahan was being a real jerk in the coaches' meeting, and Nick called him out on it, and the next thing anyone knew, Eli Pitts and some of the other assistant coaches were trying to separate the two.

Of course, you can't hide something like that, so once the media caught wind of it, it was like feeding time at the shark tank and we were holding the raw chicken. It just reinforced the public perception that we were a team in turmoil.

Interestingly, about a month later, before one of our road games, I came down to the hotel restaurant, and there were Nick and Tom having breakfast together. We're in an emotional business, where we're sometimes spending 12 hours a day together, so it was not unusual for coaches and players to occasionally have words and even fisticuffs. But we usually got over it fairly quickly.

Nick and Tom certainly did and were back to being friends before the plaster dried on the patched wall.

Thurman Thomas, who wasn't drafted until the second round, proved all the by-passers wrong by becoming the greatest ground-gainer in Bills history.
Photo by Jamie Germano/Rochester Democrat and Chronicle

THE CASE OF THE MISSING HELMET

If we had beaten the Washington Redskins in Super Bowl XXVI in Minneapolis, this incident probably would have wound up as a footnote. But because we lost, the media made a huge deal out of Thurman Thomas missing the first two plays of the game because he couldn't find his helmet.

Let me set the record straight. The Redskins had a great team that year. Even if Thurman had been in for those two plays, we still would have lost handily.

I don't know if any of us will ever know exactly what happened with Thurman's helmet that evening, but here's my take: Guys are superstitious, and I know Thurman followed a certain routine. He would lay his helmet at the end of the bench before games. This usually isn't a problem because sideline security is tight most of the time. Nobody except players, coaches, equipment men, and trainers usually get anywhere near a team's bench.

But Super Bowls are different. The pregame shows are huge, and there are hundreds of performers, celebrities, and dignitaries who surround the bench. I think that Thurman went ahead and put his helmet at the end of the bench and walked away for a moment. One of the assistant equipment guys may have picked it up because he was afraid someone might walk off with it. He probably put it under the bench for safekeeping, and then he got distracted while attending to one of the other players. When Thurman came over to get his helmet after the coin toss, it wasn't there, and he frantically started searching for it. By the time he found it, he had missed two plays.

Many columnists and commentators had fun with it by using it as metaphor for what happened to us that game, but it really had no bearing on the game. The bottom line is that the Redskins were better than we were. And to this day, I haven't seen a team that would have beaten them that night.

Thurman was a pretty sensitive guy, and the jokes about the missing helmet hounded him for a year or two after the incident. He probably could have diffused the situation by making light of it, but that wasn't Thurman's nature. Things like that really ticked him off, and he used the anger as motivation.

THE THIRD TIME'S A HARM

As we learned in our 51–3 shellacking of the Raiders during the 1991 AFC championship, a football game can avalanche out of control in a hurry. Unfortunately, we had a chance to see what it felt like to be beneath the avalanche in our 52–17 loss to the Dallas Cowboys in Super Bowl XXVII. Believe me, it doesn't feel good.

After that debacle in front of 98,374 spectators in the Rose Bowl in Pasadena, our Hall of Fame wide receiver James Lofton told reporters that "an earthquake over in Santa Monica is the only thing that would have stopped the Cowboys."

I'm not taking anything away from the Cowboys. With guys like Hall of Famers Troy Aikman and Emmitt Smith, they definitely were a great team. But there's no way in the world they were five touchdowns better than us, just as we weren't seven touchdowns better than the Raiders in 1991.

Until his knees were ravaged by injuries, Jim Kelly was nimble enough to evade his fair share of sacks. *Photo by Jamie Germano/Rochester Democrat and Chronicle*

We were our own worst enemies against Dallas, committing a Super Bowl–record nine turnovers. They cashed five of our miscues in for touchdowns, and you don't have to have a Ph.D. from MIT to realize that was the difference.

0 FOR 4

I think a lot of fans and some media had grown tired of seeing us back in the Super Bowl when we went for a third time. In fact, some nasty columnists started referring to us as "the serial killers of the Super Bowl."

But I sensed attitudes were changing toward us when we made our fourth consecutive appearance following the 1993 season. People admired our moxie. Even a guy like Terry Bradshaw—a guy with four Super Bowl rings from his Pittsburgh Steelers days—was pulling for us. Before the game in the Georgia Dome in Atlanta, he told the media, "Buffalo is a great, great football team. If I could, in my heart of hearts, have one wish, it would be that they could win this Super Bowl for Jim Kelly and Thurman Thomas and all those great fans they have. What they've accomplished is unbelievable."

Indeed, no team had ever done what we had done—made it to four consecutive Super Bowls—and people were taking notice. Of course, we also had also a chance to be a part of history that we wouldn't brag about—namely joining the Minnesota Vikings as the only franchises to go 0-4 in the Super Bowl.

It was a dubious distinction we wanted no part of, and we were hoping this would be the year. We were going to have an opportunity to redeem ourselves against that same Cowboys team that had spanked us by 35 points the year before.

Things were looking real good for a while there. We even led at the half, 13–6. But it all started to turn against us on the third play of the third quarter, when James Washington scooped up a Thurman Thomas fumble and raced 46 yards for a touchdown. Thurman felt terrible about losing the ball and went into a minifunk.

In his entire Hall of Fame career, it was the only time I ever saw Thurman down on himself. Marv, who never ever gave sideline pep talks, still regrets that he didn't make an exception and talk to Thurman after the fumble to boost his spirits. And thinking about it all these years later, I believe Thurman's lifelong friends and teammates (including me) let him down because we didn't offer him any words of encouragement either.

We never could get the momentum back after that turnover, and the Cowboys went on to beat us 30–13.

After the game, Jim Kelly told reporters, "We're going to keep going until we get it right."

I too tried to be upbeat, telling the media, "Sometimes you feel like you are just hitting your head against the wall, but as long as there is a chance for us to come back, we are going to keep fighting."

And we did, but age, injuries, and a slow, inexorable talent drain all conspired to prevent us from making a fifth run at that elusive Vince Lombardi Trophy.

We dropped to 7-9 in 1994 and missed the playoffs for the first time in seven years. We bounced back with 10-6 records each of the next two seasons but were eliminated from the playoffs each time in the first round. At the end of the '96 campaign, we were upset by the upstart Jacksonville Jaguars at Rich Stadium. It was our first postseason loss ever in the home where we once had been invincible. Jim was carted off from that game after suffering a concussion. It would be the last game he and our gritty center Kent Hull would ever play for the Bills.

SLEEPLESS NIGHTS

I don't wake up in the middle of the night thinking about our four Super Bowl losses. But I do have problems getting to sleep sometimes because of them. I must have replayed each of those games at least a hundred times in my head. I think about what I might have done differently on this play or that play that perhaps could have changed the outcome.

That may sound strange, but that feeling is human nature for athletes and coaches, particularly when your career is over and you realize you'll never get another shot at achieving your goal of winning it all. I have far more fond memories than negative memories of my career, but I'd be lying if I said I didn't want to have at least one of those opportunities to do over again.

6

BOYS WILL BE BOYS

A PRANK THAT BOMBED

I love a good prank as much as the next guy, but there was one time when my mischievous behavior nearly backfired on me.

One evening after a training camp practice at Fredonia State, I lit a four-inch firecracker that I had gotten from a friend of mine and tossed it down the hallway near the dorm room shared by Fred Smerlas and Jim Ritcher. Andre Reed was with me, and he and I hightailed it up the stairs to our room, and after about 30 seconds that felt more like 30 minutes, we heard an explosion. This was no ordinary firecracker going off. This sounded like a stick of dynamite. You could hear it all over campus. I thought, "Uh-oh, we're in deep trouble."

After a few moments, a bunch of us headed to the scene of the crime, and there were Fred and Jim, bathed in sweat, looking as if they had just gone 10 rounds in a heavyweight title bout. I thought for sure their hearts were going to jump through their chests.

Andre Reed established Bills receiving records that may never be broken.
Photo by Jamie Germano/Rochester Democrat and Chronicle

"Fred, what the [expletive] happened?" I asked, trying my best to look innocent.

"Some jerk must have thrown a bomb in here and fled the building," Fred said, still trying to catch his breath.

Things settled down after about a half an hour or so, and we all returned to our rooms. Andre and I swore each other to secrecy.

As camp progressed, I occasionally teased Fred about the bomb scare. I'd say things like, "Wow, I still can't believe how loud that bomb was."

Before we broke camp, I finally 'fessed up and told Fred I was the culprit. He was quite the prankster himself, so he took it in stride. In fact, I think he appreciated the way we had pulled it off. He and I became good friends after that. We still are.

I'm just thankful no one got hurt and that he and I lived to tell about it.

HEY ROOKIE, CAN I HAVE YOUR AUTOGRAPH?

Todd Collins was in the trainer's room during his rookie season, when Jim Kelly came up to him and asked him to autograph a Bills helmet for him. Unbeknownst to Todd, it was his own helmet he was signing. He put this big, old signature on the helmet, and Jim went back and put it back on the hook in Todd's locker.

At practice time, Todd grabbed the helmet, put in on, and headed to the field. We were stretching, when all of a sudden we noticed that Todd was wearing a helmet with his own signature on it. Guys went crazy on him, but he didn't know what the commotion was all about until he finally removed his helmet. Jim looked at him, laughed, and said, "Gotcha."

A THANKSGIVING TRADITION

Before my first Thanksgiving in Buffalo back in 1986, we were told by team officials that a nearby meat market was offering free turkeys to Bills players and coaches. All we had to do was go to the store, show some ID, and we'd be given a big bird.

Sounded like a great promotion to me, so one day after practice, Jim Kelly and I drove to the place. We told the guy that we played for the Buffalo Bills and were there to pick up our turkeys, and he looked at us like we had eyes in the middle of our foreheads. It didn't take us long to figure out that we had fallen prey to a hoax that had been played on Bills newcomers for years.

As if we didn't feel foolish enough, the whole thing had been captured on hidden camera and was shown at our team meeting the next day.

Jim and I felt like turkeys walking out of the store, but it could have been worse. The butcher/actor took it easy on us. When linebacker Ray Bentley came in, the butcher gave him a cornish game hen and told him it was a miniature turkey.

Ray said, "You don't understand. I have four kids at home." So the guy pulled out a hacksaw and instructed Ray to cut his miniature turkey into four pieces.

The funniest incident, though, occurred back in 1980 and involved former Bills running back Joe Cribbs. Joe showed up wearing his Auburn University letterman jacket with his name sown on the front. The manager told him he didn't know anything about any free turkeys, so Joe left in a huff.

The next day, in the locker room, some of the veteran players started busting on Joe, saying they bet he probably fell for that silly turkey prank.

Cribbs insisted he wouldn't be dumb enough to do that. The veterans kept egging him on, and Cribbs said, "I'll bet you $100 I didn't fall for that." Before you knew it, there were about five guys taking him up on his bet.

They then headed for the team meeting, the coaches flipped on the projector, and there, caught on film by a hidden camera, was Joe Cribbs in his monogramed Auburn letterman jacket at the counter of the meat market. Needless to say, it was a lively team meeting.

THE HARLEY BOYS

Jeeps, trucks, and sports cars were the vehicles of choice for most of the guys on the team. But offensive linemen Mitch Frerotte and Glenn Parker preferred vehicles of the two-wheel variety. They took great pride in riding their Harley-Davidsons and often would drive them to work and park them in the tunnel.

And unless you were suicidal, you made sure you didn't even breathe on their hogs.

I remember one time, ESPN's Joe Theismann was in town to do some interviews and wound up climbing on Mitch's bike without the Pit Bull's permission. As he walked up the tunnel after practice, Mitch noticed from a distance that someone was on his bike, and he went nuts.

"If you value your life you better get the [expletive] off my bike in a hurry," Mitch bellowed.

I never saw Theismann move so fast. He looked like he had seen a ghost—or maybe Lawrence Taylor coming at him on a blitz.

Other guys on our team—Freddie Smerlas, Jim Kelly, and Ruben Brown—had bikes, too, but they were never into them the way these two were.

I heard stories of Mitch and Glenn taking rides along the back roads of Western New York. Imagine what a sight that must have been—two bearded 300-pounders in black leather jackets and pants roaring through town. Some wondered whether they were Buffalo Bills players or members of Hells Angels.

JUST CALL ME "SEVE"

Backup quarterback Stan Gelbaugh and I hit it off from the moment he joined the team in 1987, and we decided to take up the game of golf together. We'd play at South Shore Country Club, several miles south of Rich Stadium. We were awful at first, but we had a lot of fun. To make things interesting, he'd pretend he was Jack Nicklaus, and I'd pretend I was Seve Ballesteros. The entire time we were on the course, I'd call him Jack and he'd call me Seve, after the famous Spanish golfer. The names stuck, so we'd call each other by our nicknames in the locker room, on the practice field, and during games. Guys began asking what that was all about, and soon everybody started calling me Seve. To this day, my old teammates and their

Steve Tasker goes airborne in an attempt to down the ball before it reaches the end zone. *Photo by Jamie Germano/Rochester Democrat and Chronicle*

wives and kids still call me by that name. In fact, I'm so attached to it that the public speaking company I own is called Seve and Associates.

WHAT'S IN A NICKNAME?

Speaking of nicknames, they've always been a part of Bills lore. And there were some great ones from the 1960s and '70s—monikers such as Golden Wheels Dubenion, The Bermuda Triangle, and The Electric Company.

Just about everyone on our team had one, and some of them were quite catchy. Darryl Talley was dubbed Talley Whacker by Fred Smerlas because he was a linebacker who could whack you really good. Shane Conlan had the largest head any of us ever saw—easily a size 8½—so we called him Buckethead, Jarhead, or Hammerhead. Ray Bentley was Darby the Dinosaur after the children's book he had written. Leon Seals was Dr. Sack, although that nickname would have been more appropriate for Bruce Smith.

Pete Metzelaars was Petey Wheat Straw because he had red, strawlike hair, but I liked his college nickname much better. Pete had attended Wabash College and was known there as the Wabash Cannonball. Offensive lineman Mitch Frerotte was called Pit Bull—a name that seemed to fit his on-field and occasional off-field demeanor, whereas Kent Hull was known simply as Tough, because he was one of those strong, dependable guys you could always count on.

Bills fans and announcers referred to Thurman Thomas as Thurmanator, a takeoff on Arnold Schwarzenegger's *Terminator* movies. But we had a different name for our star running back. Because he was built low to the ground, we called him Squatty Body or just plain Squatty.

Elijah Pitts, our running backs coach, loved Thurman. The feeling was mutual, and they enjoyed teasing one another. One day at practice, Eli, in that big booming baritone voice of his, said he heard that Thurman was suing the town of Orchard Park. We were all ears. We didn't know if he was kidding or not. Then, after a perfectly timed comedic pause, Eli said, "I understand, Thurman, you are upset because they built the sidewalks too close to your ass." All of us, Thurman included, laughed so hard we had tears in our eyes.

WINGING IT

We had no shortage of guys who could really pack away the food, but when it came to eating chicken wings, no one could hold a bone to our trainer, Eddie Abramoski.

I'd never seen anything like it. It was like watching Fred Flintstone in action. Abe would stick the wing in his mouth and suck all the meat off the bones. And nobody could keep pace with him. In a matter of minutes, he'd have a plate with bones stacked a foot high.

PARTY AT KELLY'S HOUSE

One of the best things about home wins was the postgame party at Jim Kelly's house. Those parties were always a lot of fun, and I think they did a lot in helping us put aside our petty differences and bond as a team.

Jim Kelly (12) and Bruce Smith (78) share a light moment during training camp.
Photo by Jamie Germano/Rochester Democrat and Chronicle

In 1989, when we were known as the Bickering Bills, there was a lot of tension in the locker room. Jim and Bruce and Thurman didn't hang out. I don't know if they even liked one another.

After losing that year's playoff opener in Cleveland, Jim invited guys to come over to his house. We popped open some bottles of wine, played a little pool, and shot the breeze. It was a great way to air out some of our problems away from football.

The next year, after we won our opener, Jim invited everybody over again—not just the players, but also their wives and parents and friends. Those gatherings bonded not only teammates but their families and friends as well. So when we took the field, we were playing for each other's family and friends, not just one another.

Thurman and Bruce wound up coming and everybody started getting along. Guys would bust on one another and let their hair down as a video of that day's game played on the televisions in Jim's humongous downstairs sports bar.

People would stream in and out throughout the night, and Jim kept a limo on call to take people home if they weren't in condition to drive. It was the perfect way to celebrate the victory and get to know your teammates and their families and friends in a nonstressful environment.

Jim had his people from Jim Kelly Enterprises tend bar and serve food and park cars. There were times when Jim or Bruce or Thurman or I would hop behind the bar. People danced and sang and acted silly. It was a lot of fun.

In time, Bill Polian realized what a great thing this was as far as team unity was concerned, and he would quietly slip Jim

$3,000 to help out with the bar bill. I don't know what category Bill listed that under on his expense account. All I know is that it was money well spent.

HOW MUCH IS THAT GUITAR?

After one of Jim Kelly's charity softball games at the University of Buffalo, people gathered in a nearby tent for a big auction. Rocker Eddie Van Halen was among the celebrities there, and he had donated a guitar. Jim held up the instrument on stage, but before he could start taking bids, Darryl Talley and Bruce Smith started heckling him good-naturedly. "Hey, Jim," they shouted. "Does the guitar work?" Jim said, "How do I know?" and then asked Eddie if it did.

The rocker hopped up on stage, plugged the guitar into the amp, threw about four or five switches, and played "Eruption" for about 90 seconds. It was just an absolutely awesome performance. The place went crazy.

Once Eddie finished, Jim took the mic and said, "I guess it works," and we all started laughing.

Janine Talley turned to her husband and said, "Darryl, I want that guitar." Well, Thurman Thomas overheard this and told Bruce. Word spread to other guys, and when the auction began, everyone started bidding against Darryl because we knew by the tone of Janine's voice Darryl *had* to buy the guitar. Much to his wife's delight, Darryl put up the highest bid, but not until we all made him pay thousands.

JIM'S CHARITY EVENTS

Jim Kelly's charity galas were always first-class events and a lot of fun. They set the standard for the way other athletes conducted their fundraisers. Through the years, Jim raised millions of dollars for a wide range of charities, and to this day we all attend each other's charity functions, raising millions of dollars and maintaining our lifelong friendships.

AN APPETITE FOR SUCCESS

Our offensive line was the most close-knit unit on our team, and nobody could hold a fork to those guys when it came to eating. Kent Hull and Jimmy Ritcher were the ringleaders of the group. They established a system of fines they assessed one another—$10 for a holding call, $5 for a false start, etc.—and the money would be thrown into a kitty and used when they went out on the town as a group. Of course, I don't think the money they raised from their self-imposed fines was ever nearly enough to pay their food bills. They would go to a fancy restaurant and literally order everything on the menu. It wasn't out of the ordinary for them to run up a tab in the thousands in one sitting.

Their big thing was to go to the Big Tree, which was just down the road from the stadium, after Friday practices. They'd order pizzas and wings and pitchers of beer and actually talk about that week's opponent. It was not exactly your typical unit meeting, but it worked for them, and I think those sessions helped them really bond.

Looking back on our glory years, I think our offensive line sometimes got overlooked.

Linebacker Shane Conlan (58) delivered numerous bone-crushing tackles for the Bills. *Photo by Jamie Germano/Rochester Democrat and Chronicle*

Those guys were the heart and soul of our team, and Jim and Thurman and Andre never would have had the success they had without them. You can really start to trace our demise to when Plan B free agency came about and we wound up losing Pro Bowlers Will Wolford and House Ballard.

PLAYTIME AT PARKER'S

They say you have to have a lot of little boy in you to play this game, and it's true. And there were plenty of times when we acted like little kids away from the field, especially when we had a chance to play Army. Offensive lineman Glenn Parker had a buddy who had a 30-acre farm south of Buffalo, and we'd gather there to play paintball. I swear, we had close to 40 guys there, and everybody came dressed in camouflage gear, bearing the most up-to-date paintball guns and grenades.

We'd turn it into a competition. The offense would go against the defense. Then, we'd have the little guys (the running backs, wide receivers, and defensive backs) go against the big guys (the linemen and linebackers). Sometimes we would put Shane Conlan and Fred Smerlas out there and storm their bunker.

Afterward, we'd sit around and eat the pig that Glenn had roasted and drink a ton of beer and talk and laugh about things. It was a great opportunity for guys to get to know one another in a setting other than football. I really believe, like Jim's house parties, those paintball skirmishes helped us bond as a team.

LOCKER-ROOM MUSIC

When I first arrived in the league in 1985, the oldest guys on the team usually were the ones who decided what went on the locker room, including what type of music we would blast before and after practices. But in time that changed, and the DJ honors eventually passed from the veteran guys to the biggest stars, regardless of age and experience. I remember a big argument over music raging after I joined the Bills. The battle was between country and hip-hop. After much wrangling, the two sides reached a compromise. Hip-hop would be played before practices; country afterward. Well, one day, one of the veterans got so angry about having to listen to hip-hop that he ripped the cords from the speakers. The sounds of silence didn't last long, and eventually, hip-hop bumped country completely from the locker room.

7

SQUISHING THE FISH AND OTHER OPPONENTS

THE BIGGEST RIVALRY

One of the things you learn the moment you set foot in Buffalo is that Bills fans hate the Miami Dolphins. A lot of it has to do with the Dolphins' dominance of the Bills, especially during the decade of the '70s, when Miami won all 20 games in the series. It didn't take long for the fans' dislike to be adopted by the Bills players. There was a cockiness about the Dolphins that rubbed us the wrong way. They always seemed to be shooting their mouths off in the papers, guaranteeing victories and blabbing about how they were the true kingpins of the AFC East.

We became bitter divisional rivals, and every game between us seemed to have playoff implications. In time—and I'm not overstating this—it became even more important to us, the players, than to Bills fans that we beat the Dolphins and beat them badly.

The first time I was part of a victory against them was in that initial game following the strike in 1987. We were playing them at their place, and it must have felt like the '70s all over again to Bills fans when the Dolphins jumped out to a 21–3 in the first half. But Jim went wild after halftime. He ended up outpassing Dan Marino, 359 yards to 303 yards, and we won 34–31 in overtime on a Scott Norwood field goal.

I was grateful to have a hand in the comeback. Early in the fourth quarter, I forced Miami's Scott Schwedes to fumble on a kickoff return. Scott Radecic recovered for us, and a few plays later, Jim threw a 17-yard touchdown pass to Robb Riddick.

That win was especially pleasing to Ralph Wilson, who had a winter home in the Miami area. He told reporters, "I've been bringing my friends to Bills games here for years, and they're always saying after the games, 'That's OK, Ralph. Maybe next year.' Well, I'm happy to say that 'next year' has finally arrived."

As expected, Miami coach Don Shula was not pleased with the way his team squandered a seemingly safe lead. He told his players, "You just got beat by a bad football team." Well, Marv got wind of that and filed it away for future motivation.

The Dolphins came to Rich Stadium that November and we absolutely smoked them, 27–0. Our defense was awesome. We kept Marino from throwing a touchdown pass for the first time in 31 games, snapping the second longest such streak in NFL history. More significantly, the game marked the first time the Bills had completed a season sweep of Miami since 1966.

One of our most satisfying wins in the rivalry came down there during the 1989 season opener. We won in the end when

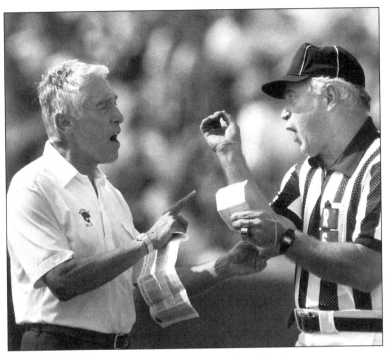

Marv Levy was known to voice his opinions to the officials.
Photo courtesy of the Rochester Democrat and Chronicle

Jim ran it in from the 2-yard line with no time remaining. That was a dagger in their hearts, because they had spent the entire off-season gearing up for that game, and the week before the opener, they were shooting their mouths off again. Their cocky little receiver, Mark Duper, told reporters, "We're going to kick their butts. I guarantee it."

One of the Bills beat reporters relayed Duper's words to me, and I told him, "Don't write a check with your mouth that your body can't cash."

They were so demoralized after Jim's game-winning touchdown they didn't even line up to defend our extra point.

I have the utmost respect for Shula. He is one of the greatest coaches in football history, but the Bills, under Marv, owned him. You can look it up. Marv wound up winning 17 of 22 head-to-head matches against the winningest coach in NFL history

A LOCKER-ROOM ATTENDANT HELPS US FILLET THE DOLPHINS

Early one season, the Dolphins came to town, and we beat them in a close game. After they boarded their bus, Art Hauret, one of our stadium attendants, was vacuuming the visitors' locker room when he came across a game-plan book that either a Miami player or a coach had left behind. He had someone take it to Marv, who filed it away. Later that season, we went down to Miami and absolutely destroyed them. It was like we knew what they were going to run before they ran it. We had never been better prepared for a game by our coaching staff.

That following Wednesday, we gathered for our team meeting. Security was very tight, and only the players and coaches and a few front-office people usually were allowed in. But for this particular meeting, we noticed Art standing in the back of the room. We thought it was kind of strange.

Marv got up in front of us and began telling us the story about how Art found the game-plan book and got it up to the coaching staff, and how it proved very valuable in helping us plot strategy for the next time we played the Dolphins. When he was done with the story, Marv pulled out a game ball with Art's name on it and presented it to him in front of the team.

We all went wild, clapping and shouting out Art's name. As was our tradition, we sang him the "Game Ball" song: "Hoo-ray for Art. Hoo-ray at last. Hoo-ray for Art; he's a horse's ass!"

You should have seen the smile on Art's face. He looked like he had died and gone to heaven.

That was the atmosphere of our team during those years. Even the secretaries and the guys who picked up the balls of wadded-up tape in the locker rooms were considered a part of the team.

The Buffalo Bills were like a big family, and Ralph Wilson contributed to that feeling. That's why, for the first Super Bowl and the three that followed, Ralph flew everybody—even the Rich Stadium security guards and their wives—to the games. It was his way of telling all of us that we were in it together.

GUYS I ADMIRED (AND SOME I FEARED)

Dan Marino owns most of the significant NFL career-passing records, but our defense wound up doing a pretty good job of containing him. We knew he wasn't going to hand it off and wasn't going to run it himself, so I think it was easier for us to game plan for him. And if you look it up, you'll see that we won more times than we lost against Dan during our run of success.

The quarterback I feared most was John Elway. He had an enormous arm that was so powerful it could even cut through the gale-force winds at Rich Stadium. He also was a guy who could hurt you with his legs, whether it was throwing on the run or tucking it under and taking off himself. John got a lot of credit for all those comebacks he engineered, but he had all those opportunities because of the poor coaching he had to overcome for three quarters. I still contend that the Broncos never would have made it to their first three Super Bowls if it hadn't been for Elway. He had to beat not only opposing defenses but an offensive game plan that didn't play to his strengths until the game was on the line.

It's like Marv used to say about comebacks, "Forget the fourth quarter, let's go out and win the game in the first quarter." And that's what we did so many times when Jim Kelly was in his prime. We'd jump out to a big lead and never look back.

Probably the greatest running back we ever went against was Barry Sanders. We didn't play him much because the Lions were in the NFC, but the few times we did see him up close and personal, he was amazing. He had a running style all his own. The unbelievable strength in his lower legs enabled him to change directions without losing any speed. Someone once said of Barry that when he was a kid and played tag, he was never it. He was as elusive as they come. He could make a highlight even out of plays that went for no gain.

Lawrence Taylor was the most imposing defensive player I ever went against. I'll never forget the first time I saw him in person. It was in the summer of 1985 and just so happened to be the first time I ever suited up for a professional football game. I was with Houston, and we were playing the Giants in the Hall of Fame exhibition game in Canton, Ohio. We were doing our pregame stretches, and the Giants came out of the locker room and jogged by us. LT went whizzing by me, and I did a double take. I said, "Holy smokes—that guy is enormous." I knew the guy was quick, but I didn't realize just how big he was. I began thinking to myself, "I'm too small to be out here doing this."

Pro Football Hall of Fame receiver James Lofton had several productive seasons for the Bills late in his career. *Photo by Jamie Germano/Rochester Democrat and Chronicle*

Speaking of big guys, I couldn't believe how huge some of the NFL safeties were. At one of the Pro Bowls, James Lofton and I were waiting to do some passing drills when we looked over and saw guys like Albert Lewis and Steve Atwater in the secondary. They were built like linebackers, 6 feet, 3 inches; 6 feet, 4 inches and 240 pounds of muscle. It could be pretty intimidating, regardless of whether you were catching one over the middle or trying to block them.

Because special teams was my main gig, I'd be remiss if I didn't mention the toughest return men I faced. Mel Gray was probably the best. He could change directions without losing speed. He was always moving forward, up the field. Other guys I worried about going the distance on a kickoff return included Clarence Verdin, Vai Sikahema, and Tim Brown.

I made one of the best plays of my career against Tim when I tackled him on a punt return in the open field to prevent a touchdown and preserve a victory. We had punted poorly, so Tim, who was scary good, had a lot of room in which to maneuver. As I was coming down on coverage, I believed that if I didn't make the tackle, he would be gone, and the game films later bore that out. I wound up grabbing his foot, and we spun around like the blades of a helicopter before landing on our butts. It was funny because we wound up sitting there, facing one another. He pointed at me as if to say, "You got me," and I just held my hands up and shrugged. A photographer captured the moment on film and it won a national award.

I'd be equally remiss, of course, if I didn't mention Deion Sanders. He never got a touchdown return on my shift, but I can honestly say he remains the best athlete I've ever seen or played against. I learned just how great he was during my second Pro Bowl. They put me in as a receiver. Jim handed the ball off to Thurman, and Deion came racing in because, like everyone else, he thought it was a running play. But Thurman pitched the ball back to Jim. Meanwhile, I was running scot-free down the field, and Jim let it fly. At that point I had about 5 or 6 yards on Deion, who was attempting to recover from the fake he fell for. I thought I had a chance for a touchdown. Not only did Deion catch up with me, he leapt over my head and made an interception. You talk about closing speed and leaping ability—nobody had it like Deion. He was one of a kind.

MAKING THE SILVER AND BLACK FEEL BLACK AND BLUE

My second-favorite team to beat was the Raiders. There was just something about them that got me going. They always seemed to have more thoroughbreds on their roster than any team in the league—guys like Marcus Allen and Tim Brown and Howie Long, absolute studs. And they had that mystique about them too, led by Darth Raider himself, Al Davis. Nobody swaggered into a stadium the way those guys did in those sharp silver and black uniforms.

Our games against them seemed to follow a pattern. They would push us around for the first half, and then we'd find a way to steal the game from them. I don't remember them ever beating us in a game that mattered, and of course, the sweetest victory in the series came in that 1990 AFC championship, when we absolutely annihilated them 51–3.

GOING TO KANSAS CITY

Everybody makes such a big deal about Oakland being the toughest place in the NFL to play because of the Hells Angels atmosphere created by crazy Raiders fans. Well, the Black Hole has nothing on Kansas City's Arrowhead Stadium. Chiefs fans are 10 times louder and 10 times meaner. They hate visiting teams with a passion I've never experienced anywhere else.

We went into Arrowhead several times during our Super Bowl runs and got our butts kicked. There was just something about that place that brought out the worst in us. We dreaded going there.

MISTAKE BY THE LAKE

Cleveland's old Municipal Stadium was by far the dumpiest place we visited. The Browns never could grow grass on the skin part of the baseball infield, so they would spray-paint the dirt green so it would look better on television. We'd come out of the game with paint stains instead of grass stains. I think our equipment guys had to order new uniforms after each time we played there.

Occasionally, the Municipal Stadium groundskeepers would put down some slabs of sod to cover the dirt, but they would never take. They were like throw rugs. You literally could pick up the slab the way you would a rug. The stadium should have had one of those "Please Replace Your Divots" signs like they do on golf courses.

The locker rooms were even worse. The drains always backed up so we showered in raw sewage. Talk about gross.

8

PRO BOWLS, "BIG" TIPS, AND A PREMATURE EXIT

MEETING THE CHIEFS' CHIEF

I grew up in a tiny town in Kansas, and one of my favorite boyhood pastimes was rooting for the Kansas City Chiefs. I'll never forget how proud I was when they beat the Minnesota Vikings in Super Bowl IV back in 1970. I loved everything about that team, including their Hall of Fame coach, Hank Stram. Hank was a brilliant strategist and a colorful character. He always wore a sharp blazer and tie on game days, and he loved to roll up a program in his hands and talk about his team's ability to "matriculate the ball down the field."

So you can imagine my excitement when I had an opportunity to meet one of my boyhood heroes while playing in a golf tournament in Hawaii the week leading up to my first Pro

Bowl appearance in 1988. I was like a little kid all over again when I shook Hank's hand and told him how much I admired him. He thanked me and asked what I was doing in Honolulu. When I told him I was there to play in the Pro Bowl, he did a double-take.

"Oh my gosh, Steve, it didn't register with me at first that you were Steve Tasker, the great special teams player," he said, embarrassed. "I thought you were just some guy's caddie, because you look so young."

I told him there was no need to apologize, because people were always confusing me for the water boy because of my baby face.

Hank and I ran into each other at various functions in the following years, and he would always greet me by saying, good-naturedly, "Hey, how's the water boy?"

WHAT A RUSH

A reporter once asked me what went on in my head as I prepared to cover the opening kickoff at a packed Rich Stadium. This is what I told him:

"It's like I'm in a soundproof booth. My concentration is so fierce I don't hear a thing. I know it sounds barbaric, but there are few feelings as good as making a big hit in football. Everyone should get a chance to experience the thrill of running downfield on a kickoff and putting a good lick on somebody in front of all those people. It's quite a rush."

AN HONEST MISTAKE

During our evenings off, some of us used to play cards with trainers Eddie Abramoski and Bud Carpenter. Because we made a lot more money as players than Abe and Bud, we would pick up the tab for the pizzas we ordered.

One night the delivery boy showed up and said the total was $15.37. I handed him a $20 bill. He gave me back my change, and I handed him 63 cents and pocketed the four dollars. For some reason, I didn't even think that it would have been nice if I had given him a bigger tip.

After he left, Abe and the other guys started hammering me for not tipping him more. They went on for about 20 minutes busting my chops. I deserved it.

The next night, we were playing cards again, and a different delivery boy showed up with our pizza. John Kidd had left a $20 bill on the table and was in the bathroom when the delivery was made, so I picked up the bill and handed it to the kid. I told him to keep the change, and he was all excited. He said, "Oh man, I love delivering to the Bills, because you guys are such big tippers."

Without missing a beat, I told him, "Son, we pride ourselves on that."

Abe and Bud started laughing so hard they were crying.

To this day, Abe loves telling the story of what a big tipper I am as long as it's somebody else's money.

FIRST PRO BOWL

Walt Corey, our defensive coordinator, was the guy who let me know I had made the Pro Bowl for the first time back in 1987. I was so overwhelmed in the team meeting that I started to cry. I put my head down so that guys wouldn't see the tears.

To this day, I still get goose bumps thinking about it. You have to remember that I was a guy who considered every single down I played in the NFL a bonus. I regarded myself as nothing more than a role player, a guy picked up off the waiver wires holding on for dear life every Sunday, which was why getting picked for an honor like that was way beyond my comprehension.

And back then Pro Bowl invitations were based solely on a vote of your peers—the fans and media weren't involved—so that made it all the more special. It meant I had made an impression among the guys I locked horns with each Sunday. They were the guys who truly understood what it took to play at this level.

The night I found out about my selection, Sarah and I went to a Christmas party in Buffalo. I was just beaming the entire evening. I couldn't wipe the smile off my face.

It remains absolutely the biggest thrill I've had in football.

SURGERY THAT MADE ME FASTER

I hurt my left knee during my rookie season in 1985, and for the next several seasons, I had to tape it up like a mummy because it was so unstable. Finally, after the 1988 season, I decided enough was enough. I underwent surgery on it and

Steve Tasker is congratulated by Bills tight end Keith McKeller after a touchdown reception. *Photo courtesy of the Rochester Democrat and Chronicle*

wound up becoming faster and quicker. I can thank our team physician, Dr. Richard Weiss, and an anonymous dead man for the additional speed.

Dr. Weiss suggested we try a new medical procedure in which they take part of a leg muscle from a cadaver and staple it to the top and bottom of your medial collateral ligament. I didn't understand what the heck he was talking about, but it sounded worth a shot. My knee had been so unreliable that I figured any alternative other than the status quo had to be better.

I worked diligently to rehab the knee following the surgery, and when I reported to training camp before the 1989 season, I could tell that I had a gear I hadn't possessed before. I was keeping pace with guys like J. D. Williams—guys who could absolutely fly. Even Marv Levy noticed. He asked, "Steve, is it just my imagination, or are you running faster?" I told him straight-faced: "Coach, I get faster every year." He's like, "Yeah, OK. Sure, Steve."

FOR A DAY, THE BEST OF THE BEST

One of my biggest thrills was when I was named Most Valuable Player of the Pro Bowl in 1992. I forced a fumble on a punt return, blocked a field goal, and made four special teams tackles that, taken together, must have swayed the voters. That's the thing about Pro Bowls. You have a bunch of All-Stars out there, and everybody is playing a limited amount of time, so you don't necessarily have to throw five touchdown passes or make 25 tackles to win MVP honors. If you make a few pivotal plays, your chances are pretty good.

On the forced fumble, I actually got cold cocked by one of the NFC blockers. I swear I must have rolled about six times before coming to a stop. Because I was one of the only full-time special teams player on the punt coverage unit, I knew I had to get back on my feet ASAP and continue chasing the return man. I wound up closing in on him from behind and popped the ball out of his hands just as he cut back. It wound up in our punter's hands, and we cashed the second chance in for a touchdown.

My other momentum-changing play came on a Morten Anderson field-goal attempt in the second half. When the NFC broke the huddle, Mike Singletary and Reggie White lined up to block me. Singletary, the Chicago Bears Pro Bowl linebacker, started talking trash to me as he got into his stance. He said, "You better bring it, baby. You better bring it."

Well, they snapped the ball, and I put a fake on Singletary, and he missed me by a mile. That gave me an open path to the ball, and I wound up blocking the kick with my armpit. One of my teammates, Terry McDaniels, picked up the bouncing ball and took it in for a score.

Toward the end of the game, I made a big tackle on Deion Sanders, and we wound up winning by a field goal in overtime.

About ten days later, Sarah and I were at a conference for NFL players and their wives. Singletary and his wife were there, and when he saw me, he chuckled and gave me a big hug. He said, "You know, you should really give me your Pro Bowl MVP trophy, seeing as how I'm really responsible for you receiving it."

Some people asked if I got a car for being Pro Bowl MVP. I didn't, but the trophy I received sits in my office and is one of my most prized possessions. There was a time when I didn't know whether I was good enough to play a single down in the

NFL. And there I was, holding my Pro Bowl MVP trophy. For one fleeting day, I could say I was the best of the best. That was pretty cool.

ZEBRA PHOBIA

Marv Levy was one of the most eloquent coaches in the history of football—a true gentleman. But on game day, mild-mannered Marv was known to occasionally blister a referee's ear with an F-bomb or two.

I had a really bad temper on the sidelines too, and nothing set me off like a bad call or a missed call. I don't know why. Maybe I had a bad experience with a zebra as a kid. I just had no tolerance for mistakes by referees. It's almost like I couldn't accept the fact that they were human, and just like us players, they occasionally made mistakes. To this day, as a father, I can hardly control myself at my kid's athletic events when a ref makes a bad call.

In retrospect, I'm surprised I didn't get flagged for unsportsmanlike conduct for baiting the officials. If they blew a call, I would needle them big time. I'd keep riding them until the point just before they were going to yank the flag, and then I would shut up. I know I could never be a coach because I would go nuts every time a ref missed something out there. It's definitely irrational behavior on my part, because I realize that the vast majority of the time, the officials get it right.

CALLING IT QUITS

Many of the guys I played with—guys like Jim Kelly and Kent Hull—were gone by the time I began my final season in

1997. As I looked around the locker room during training camp in Fredonia that August, I couldn't help but notice all the strange, young faces. That's not to say that I didn't enjoy playing and being with the new guys, because I did. But it just wasn't the same feeling I had during the so-called good old days.

We definitely were in a rebuilding mode in '97, and after having experienced so much success for so long, it was really tough for me to handle a 6-10 record and a fourth-place finish in a division we used to own. When we took the field, we'd get beat by teams we used to mop the place with. It was sad to see how far we had fallen.

Perhaps the lowest point came during a late-season game against the Chicago Bears. They beat us 20–3 at Soldier Field. It was the most pathetic game I'd ever been involved in. Mind you, this is from a guy who played at Northwestern University during the era of a 34-game losing streak. We were so bad on offense that day we couldn't get out of our own way. I thought to myself afterward, "We are the worst team in football right now. We just lost to a team that three or four years ago wouldn't have belonged on the same field as us."

Even sadder for me was the realization that I no longer was the player I had been. Injuries and mileage on my body had taken their toll. They prevented me from training the way I wanted to and needed to. That, in turn, prevented me from being as good as I wanted to be. It's a huge blow to an athlete's pride to go out and play when he isn't good anymore.

The press conference announcing my retirement was pretty emotional for me. I had a tough time not getting choked up. I told reporters that day, "There were three things I wanted to accomplish as a professional athlete—I wanted to be a guy my teammates loved to have on their team; I wanted to be a guy who my opponents wished they had on their team; and I wanted to be a guy that the fans loved to watch. I don't know if I accomplished any of those three, but I thank God for the gift and the opportunity he gave me to try."

I think Marv was as sad as I was that day. He had been my mentor, and I had been his dutiful student, and we both shared a passion for the importance of special teams. The kicking units had been his baby ever since he broke into the NFL coaching ranks in the late 1960s, and I may be biased, but I believe he was ahead of his time as far as realizing how the kicking teams could significantly influence a game.

He paid me an incredible compliment that day when he told reporters I was "the greatest special teams player to ever play the game." He added, "I don't think anyone in the history of the game has played his position any better than Steve has." I don't believe that's true, but it was the greatest accolade I received during my football career because it came from a man whom I grew to love and respect.

Looking back, I'm proud to say I was in Buffalo for all but a few days of the Marv Levy era. I was the first player he acquired, and we both wound up retiring from the game at the same time. I couldn't have scripted it any better.

A CURTAIN CALL TO REMEMBER

I wasn't going to announce my retirement until after the 1997 season, but my plans changed just before our home finale against the Jacksonville Jaguars. My buddy, Jim Kelly, who was working as an NFL analyst for NBC at the time, became aware of my intentions and forced my hand. I had spilled the beans on his retirement the year before, so he joked that it was payback time. In reality, Jim was just trying to do me a favor. He said if I didn't let the Bills fans know ahead of time, I'd be cheating them because they would want to share the special moment with me.

Jim told me if I didn't go public with it, he would break the news on that Sunday's telecast. I talked it over with Sarah, and she agreed with Jim. Though I didn't want to call attention to my decision, I reluctantly contacted Bills public relations director Scott Berchtold, and we held a press conference at the stadium the day before our game against Jacksonville.

I owe Jim big time, because my home finale wound up being an unforgettable experience for me. After the Bills offensive players were introduced that Sunday before kickoff, my name was announced over the PA system, and I came running out of the tunnel to a thunderous ovation. On the JumboTron, they showed a montage of memorable plays from my career. It was really cool. I now have it on DVD, and my kids get a kick out of watching it on occasion.

Unbeknownst to me, Sarah had arranged for my parents, Gordon and JoAnn Tasker, along with my three brothers—Keith, David, and Paul—and their wives to attend the game.

We wound up losing to the Jags, but that couldn't put a damper on things. At the end of the game, Sarah and four of our children—Deacon, Annie, Luke, and Tap—came out of the stands and accompanied me on one final journey off the field. Sarah was seven months pregnant with our fifth child, Jacob, at the time.

As I walked through the tunnel, I looked up and heard fans shouting my name. I thought to myself, "I'm going to miss this a lot." And I have.

That night, we held the team party at my house, and a bunch of the guys showed up. I have a picture of me with Jim, Bruce, Thurman, Andre, and six or seven other teammates standing on my snow-covered deck, smoking cigars. It remains one of my most prized possessions.

A CURTAIN CALL TO FORGET

I played my final NFL game on December 20, 1997, at historic Lambeau Field in Green Bay . . . or should I say I played my final three minutes that day, because that's how long my work shift lasted, thanks to a bonehead move on my part.

Here's what happened: I was back to field a punt after the Packers went three-and-out on their first series, and the ball sailed over my head. As it bounced toward the end zone, it supposedly glanced off our cornerback, Ray Jackson, and the Packers recovered for a touchdown. I didn't believe it hit Ray, so I sprinted toward the referee to try to convince him of his error. But while doing so, I accidentally bumped one of the officials. I was so focused on arguing my case about the ball not having hit Ray that I didn't realize what I had done.

The referee had no choice but to jettison me, because that was the rule. I couldn't argue with it, because any physical contact with an official is an automatic ejection.

As I jogged toward the locker room, I felt like a fool. I said to myself, "Nice curtain call, Tasker, you doofus. Three freaking minutes and you're done."

The day had begun so gloriously for me. In honor of my final game, Marv sent me out by myself for the coin toss. Brett

Favre and Reggie White were among the Packer captains out there, and they shook my hand and gave me hugs. Even the officials came up to shake my hand.

When I reached the visitor's locker room, the attendant—a kindly old guy dressed head to toe in Packers regalia—asked me what had happened. After I told him, he said, "Ah, man, come over here and get a sandwich."

So I took my helmet off and sat there with him, eating a sandwich, drinking a Dr. Pepper, and watching the game on television. Talk about bizarre.

I went into a nearby office and closed the door during halftime so I wouldn't have to talk to any of my teammates. After they went out for the third quarter, I showered and changed. When the game ended, I was nervous because I figured my teammates were going to rip into me. Jerry Ostrowski, one of our offensive linemen, was the first one in. He looked at me, looked away, then looked at me again. He started grinning at me and said, "Steve Tasker, you are the man. I want to go out just like you did. I'm going to end my career by getting thrown out of the game. That was awesome."

I couldn't help but laugh. That broke the tension and helped make an embarrassing situation more bearable.

Later, I went up to Marv and apologized to him. He told me not to worry and said that it was a bad call and that we'd talk later.

Marv had a rule then that if you got thrown out of a game, you were docked a percentage of your paycheck based on how much of the game you had missed. I was making a lot of money at the time, and I thought because I played only three minutes, I probably was going to lose all the money from that week. Fortunately for me, they waived the fine.

We got trounced 31–21 by the defending Super Bowl champs that day, and I wound up being a sidebar. I took my medicine with the media in the postgame interviews. I was wrong, and I felt like a fool. It wasn't exactly the ending I had envisioned for my career.

TRANSITIONING INTO REAL LIFE

It's been said that an athlete dies two deaths. The first death occurs when his career ends, and the second one occurs when his life ends.

The typical career span of a professional football player is something like three or four years, so that means most guys are done while still in their 20s. I was blessed to have played into my 30s. But I knew from the moment I played my first down in the NFL that I could be just one snap away from retirement, so I began early making plans for my life after football.

I had majored in communications at Northwestern with an eye on going into broadcasting. While playing for the Bills, I spent time cohosting a morning show on a Buffalo television station, and I did a variety of radio call-in shows. It was good preparation for my current career as an NFL analyst with CBS and host of a weekly Bills television show.

Although there's nothing careerwise that can equal the high I experienced playing football, I've found broadcasting to be incredibly challenging and fulfilling. It's enabled me to remain involved in the game I love, and I think that has helped in my transition from one career to the next.

The good thing is that I leave the broadcast booth after a game without feeling the physical and emotional aches and pains I experienced as a player. The bad thing is that I miss the adrenaline rush I felt as a player after a win and the camaraderie with my teammates.

I've been blessed because I've been able to find something rewarding to do after hanging up my helmet and pads. Sadly, some guys don't make the adjustment when the cheering stops and they have to enter the "real" world. They can't find anything they like to do other than playing football, or they don't make preparations for their postplaying career far enough in advance.

9

EXTRA POINTS

CARRYING THE TORCH
FOR BUFFALO

O nce we started winning in the late 1980s, my teammates and I quickly learned that we weren't just playing for the Bills but for the entire city of Buffalo and beyond. Because Buffalo is the third smallest market in the NFL, it's different there than in most other places. In New York, LA, Chicago, Washington, and Boston, there are so many sports teams to root for and a much larger population base from which to draw. In Buffalo, the Bills are *the* game in town, and when things are going well with the team, you can feel the positive vibes every place you go.

Buffalo is a great place to live, but there's a little bit of an inferiority complex here, because the city has taken so much grief for its weather and floundering economy. So when we were winning the majority of our games and going to the four consecutive Super Bowls, you could see the pep in people's steps. We were a source of pride, a chance for Buffalonians to puff out their chests.

Conversely, when things went bad, we noticed people being down in the dumps. I remember reading about a study someone did that documented how worker productivity in Buffalo and the surrounding areas declined the day after one of our losses (i.e., there would be a higher rate of absenteeism, etc). The malaise came to be known as "Blue Mondays."

That's how ingrained the Bills were and are in Western New York's collective psyche.

And I think the players welcomed that passion from the community. It made many of us believe that we were playing for a cause greater than ourselves. We were carrying the torch for Buffalo.

The support we received was truly amazing. Despite our small market size, large stadium (it held more than 80,000 fans back then), and challenging late-fall weather, we sold out most of our games and wound up setting a single-season NFL attendance record. For six consecutive seasons we led the league in attendance.

In 1992, Ralph Wilson did a classy thing when he honored the fans by placing the "12th Man" on the Rich Stadium Wall of Fame. He was telling them that they were a huge part of our success too.

From 1988 through 1995, the Bills led the National Football League in attendance six times. *Photo courtesy of the Rochester Democrat and Chronicle*

PULLING THE PLUG ON THE LOUD HOUSE

In the years leading up to our first Super Bowl, Rich Stadium was so loud you couldn't hear the guy standing next to you on the sideline even when he was screaming at you. Sometimes the only way you could communicate was by reading lips. The place held 80,000 spectators back in those days, and it really rocked on game day. You could feel the tremors.

Things started to change, though, when they began modernizing the stadium following Super Bowl XXV in January 1991. The huge JumboTron television screen they installed on the scoreboard side of Rich had a major effect on the way fans viewed the game in person. Instead of having this continuous roar throughout the game, people stopped cheering between plays so they could watch the replays. Certainly, there have been moments since the installation of the JumboTron and the scores of new luxury suites when the fans have been as loud and as frenzied as before. But the roar no longer is nonstop, and it never will be again.

FUELING OUR SUPER BOWL RUN

The run we had was fantastic, but eventually it took its toll on us mentally and physically. Counting the Super Bowls, we played 13 additional games between 1990 and 1994. That's just three games shy of another full season, so we essentially played five seasons in a four-year span. That's an awful lot to ask of your mind and body, and in time it caught up with us, as it would have with any team.

I think one of the reasons we were able not only to survive but flourish for as long as we did was Rusty Jones. He was our strength and conditioning coach, and as far as I'm concerned, there is nobody better at what he does. Rusty was way ahead of the competition as far as realizing the importance of body composition and nutrition.

I also credit Marv's handling of us. He knew he had a veteran team, so there was no need to run us into the ground during training camp or even the regular season. While other teams were running on fumes heading into the playoffs, we always seemed to have plenty of gas left in our tanks. We can thank Marv and Rusty for that.

THE MOURNING AFTER

Legendary coach Vince Lombardi once said, "Dancing is a contact sport; football is a collision sport." Man, was he ever right.

Mornings after games, I'd roll out of bed feeling as if I had been in a violent car wreck the day before. My whole body would be tender. I'd feel as if I was 25 going on 85.

I used to do a morning show with one of the Buffalo television stations, and there were times when I would show up the Monday following a game with bruises on my face or a cast on my wrist or my leg wrapped up like that of a mummy. I could have been a poster child for the walking wounded.

I can't imagine what Thurman Thomas felt like. I might have just a few collisions a game, but as a running back, Thurman was forced to endure hits virtually every time he touched the ball, which might be as many as 25 to 30 times a game.

I also can't imagine what Jim Kelly must have felt like after some of those hellacious sacks. Quarterbacks can be sitting ducks. There are times when they literally don't know what hit them—times when raging, 300-pound pass rushers come in from a quarterback's blind side and pancake him against turf that's often about as forgiving as a slab of concrete.

The amazing thing—and one that fans and the media often take for granted—is that these guys keep getting up and performing, sometimes as if nothing has happened. If a person on the street took a hit like that, he'd be out of work for weeks. For football players, it's just one of the occupational hazards. You shake it off and play the next play, then pay for it the next day.

You learn early on that you have to play with pain, but you can't play with fear. The minute you start worrying about getting hit or getting hurt out there, is the minute you should quit. You need to have complete concentration on the task at hand, whether it's catching a pass or shedding off a blocker. You really have to put the blinders on in order to succeed, and you have to learn how to bounce back from injuries.

During my 12 years in the NFL, I required five knee surgeries, broke my hands or fingers nine times, incurred a stress fracture in my vertebrae, and had my cornea scratched. Despite all of the breaks, rips, strains, cuts, and bruises I had to endure, I feel remarkably good at age 44. I realize, though, that I'm one of the lucky ones, because a lot of guys leave football with debilitating injuries and conditions that will affect them the rest of their lives.

I credit good fortune and our trainers, Eddie Abramoski and Bud Carpenter, for keeping me in one piece long enough to play as long as I did. I trusted Abe and Bud with my career and my health, and they never steered me wrong. There were times when I attempted to twist their arms to let me get back out there, and they didn't budge if they thought I was at risk for more serious injury. I always believed they had my best interests at heart.

CONCUSSIONS

There was a Monday night game in San Francisco when I got smacked in the back of the head and felt a little strange. My teammate, Billy Brooks, came up to me and asked me if I was OK, and I said, "I don't know." He told me to go to the sideline for a play, and our trainer, Bud Carpenter, asked me a number of questions such as "Where are we?" and "What day of the week is it?" and I answered everything fine.

I went back into the game, and Jim called a play that he'd called a hundred times, and I asked him, "What am I supposed to do on that play?" He looked at me as if I was crazy and immediately sent me back to the sideline.

I spent the rest of the game with an ice pack on the back of my neck. That's the way it is with concussions. Sometimes you are in la-la land right away, and sometimes it's a delayed reaction like the one I had in San Fran that night.

The next day, I was in the team meeting watching films of the game, and I saw myself making a catch against the 49ers that I had no memory of. After that game, I had talked with some close friends of mine in San Francisco while waiting for the team bus, and the next day I had no recollection of that either.

That was scary.

PREGAME RITUALS

I remember sitting in the locker room before playing my first game with the Bills midway through the 1986 season, and I heard this guy throwing up violently in the bathroom. I turned to one of my teammates and said, "Who is that losing lunch?" and he said, "Oh, that's Jim Kelly."

I said, "Geez, he must be really sick. Is he going to be able to play?" And the guy told me, "Yeah, he'll play. That's just Jim's pregame ritual. If he doesn't hug the porcelain bowl before a game, he doesn't feel like he's ready."

I thought to myself, "Man, that's really sick," no pun intended.

Jim was pretty superstitious. He had routines he wouldn't deviate from. For instance, he and Frank Reich always had to have lunch together the day before a game. Just him and Frank, nobody else.

After he threw up on game days, Jim would say a prayer in front of his locker, and he would make sure that he and I always walked down the tunnel side by side before taking the field for pregame warmups. We'd tap fists, and I'd say to him, "Jim, no matter what happens, just keep slinging it."

I normally didn't arrive at the stadium on game day until about three hours before kickoff, but some guys got there so early I think they opened up the place. And there were guys such as Chris Spielman who, I swear, must have slept in the locker room the night before a game.

One time, I wound up going to the stadium really early on game day. It must have been about 7:15 in the morning, and the place was empty except for Chris, who was lying in front of my locker, watching television. He was taped and had everything on except his shoulder pads and helmet. I wasn't really surprised, because that was just Chris being Chris. He loved playing football as much as any player I've ever known. Kickoff for him was like Christmas morning for a little kid. He couldn't wait for the game to get started.

SUPER BOWL JOKES

The fact we lost four consecutive Super Bowls has spawned a lot of jokes. Some of them are quite cruel, but I've tried to keep things in perspective and not let them bother me. Besides, sometimes you have to laugh about things in order not to cry.

Here are some of the ones I've heard ad nauseam:

Bills stands for "Boy, I Love Losing Super Bowls."

It takes four *L*s to spell *Bills*.

Q: What do you call a Buffalo Bill with a Super Bowl
    ring?
A: A thief.

Q: How many Buffalo Bills does it take to win a Super
    Bowl?
A: Nobody knows, and we may never find out.

One of the reasons my teammates and I pull so hard for the current Bills is that we long for the day when they do win a Super Bowl and we can stop being a punch line.

GAME BALLS

It's been a long-standing tradition to reward players with a commemorative football following a victory. I have a bunch of them from my years with the Bills, and they're among my most prized possessions because they evoke such fond memories. The team does a great job with them. They paint your name, the team logo, the score, and the date of the game on the panels. The balls are very sharp looking.

Normally only a few were awarded after each victory, and the captains or coaching staff usually decided the honorees. Jim Kelly, Thurman Thomas, and Bruce Smith were so good that we could have presented them with balls after virtually every victory, but to their credit, they urged us to spread them around. I thought it was a great gesture on their part, because it helped make all 47 guys on the roster feel as if they were contributing members to our success. It was one of those subtle things that helped build team unity and a sense of belonging.

I remember playing the Jets in New York on Monday night, and it happened to be Ralph Wilson's birthday. So, following the victory, we did a "Hooray for Ralph" chant and presented him with a ball from the players and coaches. He was so thrilled. He looked like a 10-year-old blowing out candles on a cake.

CELEBRITY FOLLOWING

Though we didn't play in Los Angeles or New York, we did develop a sizable celebrity following nationwide. Some of the celebs—such as Tim Russert of NBC's *Meet the Press* and new Supreme Court Justice John Roberts—rooted for us because they had either grown up in Buffalo or had spent some time living there during their formative years. Others, such as golf star Phil Mickelson, adopted us because they liked our never-say-die attitude. And still others—such as Donald Trump, Meatloaf, and Eddie Van Halen—jumped on our "fanwagon" because of their friendships with Jim Kelly.

Of all our celebrity fans, none was more gung ho than Chris Berman, the ESPN sportscaster people fondly refer to as Boomer. For some reason, we captured Boomer's fancy during our glory years, and he would really get into it while showing highlights of our games. I think he, like Mickelson, really appreciated our resiliency and liked how everyone—from Jim to the last guy on our roster—contributed to our success.

During his telecasts, Boomer often told viewers nationwide that "Nobody circles the wagons like the Buffalo Bills." It became our calling card, and we absolutely loved it because we believed it was true. The worse the odds, the better we seemed to perform.

Over time, Boomer became more than just a journalist to many of us. He became our friend. Whenever he was in town for work or speaking engagements, he would get together with Jim and some of the guys. He even went to Kelly's house for a few of our postgame parties. We enjoyed listening to him deliver some of his signature phrases such as, "He . . . could . . . go . . . all . . . the . . . way!" or "Back-back-back-back-back-back-back-back. Oh, Doctor!"

He was a lot of fun, and we enjoyed having him on our side. But we also knew the airtime we received wasn't because of our friendship with him but rather because we were winning so often. Once we started losing, we didn't see nearly as many Bills highlights on ESPN or elsewhere.

O.J.'S TRAVAILS

O. J. Simpson was in Buffalo often during our glory years to do features and game coverage for NBC, and each time he returned it was one big, warm homecoming. The Juice loved Buffalo, and Buffalo loved The Juice.

He had turned in some of the most electrifying performances in NFL history while playing running back for the Bills during the 1970s, and his infectious personality and Hollywood good looks helped him gain even greater fame as a product pitchman, actor, and broadcaster.

While in Hawaii for my first Pro Bowl in 1988, my wife, Sarah, got O.J.'s autograph. It was the only time she ever asked anyone for an autograph, and that underscored to me just how popular O.J. was and how his appeal extended well beyond his football-playing skills.

Like everyone else, we were shocked and saddened in June of 1994 by the news that he had been charged in the deaths of his ex-wife and her boyfriend. It was so unbelievable, so bizarre, so surreal, and it ripped the heart out of Buffalonians, who had come to consider O.J. a member of the family.

MEDIA RELATIONS

I never read the sports section of the local newspapers while I was playing, and I tried not to listen to sports talk shows on the radio or watch local sports telecasts. Not that I had anything against the writers or broadcasters who covered us. In fact, I enjoyed being interviewed by them and getting to know them, and from what I've been told, they were very good to me with their coverage throughout my playing career. Plus, I understood they had a job to do, just like we did.

It's just that I believed what was written or said about me couldn't do anything to make me a better player and couldn't contribute anything to helping us win, and those were the only things that concerned me.

However, most of the guys on our team did read and listen and watch. Some of them could recite verbatim every word that was written or spoken about them. And a lot of times they allowed a comment to get under their skin. I think the media coverage helped fan the flames of "The Bickering Bills" soap opera in 1989. There was a lot of tension in the locker room that season, and some of the things said on television and in the newspaper contributed to differences between players and their families.

I understand that people in the media had their jobs to do, and I tried to cooperate with them at all times. I just think I was better off not knowing how they perceived me or my teammates and coaches.

A PLAYBOOK CALLED THE BIBLE

About 10 of us would gather with our wives each Thursday night to study the Bible.

Frank Reich, now an ordained minister in North Carolina, often led the discussions, which centered on the teachings of the good book and our devotion to our Christian faith. While the gatherings were religious in nature, they also had a social component to them. We all became close friends. It's fun to look back and track how our families have shared so many of life's momentous events together: marriages, births, deaths. Heck, we even seemed to purchase our pets at the same time. No matter how much time passes, our families remain close with one another. A lifelong bond was formed from those gatherings.

HAND-HOLDING

Twice in my Bills career, my teammates and I had held hands along the sideline during a pivotal moment of the game, and although it was a nice show of solidarity, it did nothing to sway things in our favor.

The first time was during the final drive of our 1989 playoff game against the Browns in Cleveland. We were holding hands as Jim Kelly drove us down the field, only to see victory slip through the fingers of Ronnie Harmon in the corner of the end zone.

The second time we held hands was before Scott Norwood's 47-yard field-goal attempt in Super Bowl XXV. After that kick went awry, I made a decision that I was never going to do that again during a game.

RELATING TO CURRENT-DAY BILLS

Having played the game earns retired players credibility the instant they walk into a locker room. There's a connection between us and the current players. They respect the fact that we experienced and endured the gridiron battles. They know we understand the highs and the lows that come from playing the game.

And the respect usually is mutual. Yes, there may be some things guys from my day might not like—such as the rash of trash-talking and overexuberant celebrations. But for the most part, we "old-timers" respect and appreciate the current players just as guys such as Jack Kemp and Billy Shaw and Joe DeLamiell respected and appreciated us.

I know I always enjoyed it when Bills from the past visited. It was fun to listen to the old stories. I think it made us realize that we were part of a special tradition in Buffalo. It connected the past and the present.

I guess the only thing we didn't want to hear when we were playing was some former player telling people that our team couldn't carry his team's jockstrap. It had the same effect as a parent telling a kid, "Back in my day, we used to walk 10 miles barefoot through the snow just to get to school." Nobody wants to hear it.

It's interesting and perhaps a tad unfair, but when I look at a current Bills player, I view him in the context of how he might fit with the teams I played on. How could we have used him on our offense or our defense or our special teams? What kind of personality does he have? Could I have lived with him in our locker room?

I guess the best compliment I could give a current Bill would be to tell him, "You definitely would have been a welcome addition to our Super Bowl teams."

PERFORMANCE ENHANCERS

The closest I ever came to taking steroids was in college. I didn't know what it would take to make it to the NFL, and like many other college players, I was thinking it would be great to be able to take something that would help me get stronger and play better. I decided not to, and I'm happy I didn't. I'd love to tell you that the reason I didn't take them is because I'm a person of high morals and thought they were wrong. But the truth of the matter is that I was just a college student struggling to get by financially, and I flat-out couldn't afford them.

The sad thing, as we've seen from the baseball and Olympic scandals, is that steroids are as good as advertised. They work. But there also can be tragic side effects from their usage (think of Lyle Alzado's sad story). They are wrong to use because they lead to an unlevel playing field and, of course, because they are illegal.

I learned at my first minicamp with the Houston Oilers in 1985 that I didn't need any performance enhancers in order to play. I discovered that I was good enough to hold my own with my God-given abilities and a lot of hard work. I was as fast as most guys out there, and I lifted a ton of weights to improve my strength.

I do believe that when I came into the league, the vast majority of big guys—linemen, linebackers, fullbacks among them—were on some form of anabolic steroid. Performance enhancers were prevalent, but I don't believe they are anymore. I'm not naive enough to think that there aren't some guys still out there beating the system with designer drugs such as THG, but I believe the NFL, starting with its crackdown in 1989, is doing a better job than most other sports leagues in addressing the issue. And I think the BALCO scandal, which involved several prominent baseball players, has deterred even more athletes in all sports from trying to cheat.

CHEAP SHOTS

Guys such as Jack Tatum, Conrad Dobler, and Bill Romanowski had reputations for being dirty players. But I think people would be surprised to learn how few cheap-shot artists there really are out there. Players have a code that they abide by, and if you are out there attempting to ruin someone's body (and therefore his livelihood) with dirty tactics, you can bet the mortgage that there will be retaliation.

You hear stories from the past where Buddy Ryan put a bounty on an opposing player's head. He'd tell his guys, "I'll give a thousand to the guy who knocks so-and-so out of the game."

I really don't think anyone could get away with that today. With free agency, players are constantly on the move, so there aren't any secrets anymore.

WEATHER ADVANTAGE

A lot of people thought cold-weather teams like the Bills were at a disadvantage when they played late-season games in warm-weather cities such as Miami. The thinking was we would wilt under the heat because we hadn't experienced it in months. But I never felt that way. I loved going to South Florida in December, and so did my teammates.

Rusty Jones, in my mind the best strength and conditioning coach in NFL history, would make sure we were properly hydrated the week leading up to our trip down south, so the heat never posed a problem. If anything, it was so invigorating for us to arrive in Miami and not have to worry about bundling up in thermal underwear and plastic tops and several pairs of socks. We felt so light and fast out there on the field in Miami or Southern California, it was almost as if we were playing in the nude.

Conversely, I always thought it was an advantage for us to host a warm-weather team in December. We were prepared for the cold conditions because we had been practicing and playing in them for weeks. It was second nature to us.

Our visitors, though, weren't used to the snow and the wind chills, and they often didn't know how to dress to protect themselves from the elements. A lot of it was mental, because the media would spend the entire week asking them about how they were going to handle the cold and wind at Rich Stadium. You'd read stories about how the Dolphins or the Raiders were packing 2,700 extra pounds of silk thermal underwear for their trip to Buffalo. It just gave them an additional thing to worry about.

A RINGING ENDORSEMENT

I'm one of the few guys from our Super Bowl teams who still wears an AFC championship ring. I wear the one from our fourth AFC title, because it represents our fourth consecutive trip to the Super Bowl—a feat unprecedented in NFL history. Of course, people will be quick to remind you that we also are the only team ever to lose four Super Bowls in four years, which is why most of my teammates won't wear any of them. They don't wanted to be reminded that we were 0-4 in the Big Game.

It's kind of sad, really, when you think about it. We finished second best in the world at what we did for four straight years, yet we're regarded as losers.

I've had guys who won the Super Bowl see the ring on my finger and start busting on me. They try to get my goat by showing me their ring and asking me if I want to try it on. It really doesn't bother me. I'm proud of what we did and how we kept coming back. We could have folded up like an accordion after the second Super Bowl, but we didn't.

Yeah, I would love to have won one, but it didn't happen. In a strange way, it has made us more distinctive, and as time goes on, I think people are appreciating more and more just how difficult and remarkable it is to get there four straight times. Even the modern-day New England Patriots—as great as they are—weren't able to do that. Yes, they won three in four years, but they were 5-11 the season they didn't make it.

I wear the ring proudly not because of the games we won, and certainly not because of the games we lost. Perhaps as you read this book, you realized why I'm so proud to have that fourth ring on my finger. I wear it to honor the men I played with and the era it represents.

I believe Ralph Wilson has the best take on our Super Bowl run. He said we were the NFL's silver medalists for four straight years. I kind of like the sound of that.

Celebrate the Heroes of Professional Football
in These Other NEW and Recent Releases from Sports Publishing!

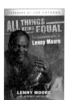